BUILDING YOUR BUSINESS THROUGH RELATIONSHIPS

CONTACTS CONNECTIONS COLLABORATION AND CRISIS

KAREN HOFFMAN, BOBBI LINKEMER

GATEWAY TO DREAMS

ISBN: 978-1-7377603-0-6

Cover design: Mitzi Hoffman

Written by Karen S. Hoffman and Bobbi Linkemer

with Shelly Snow Pordea

CONTENTS

How to stay connected

How to make connections deeper

Leveraging connections to build your business

Share with others what you are looking for

Conclusion

Differences Between

Contacts and Connections

How To Become A Connector

Choosing the Right Social Media

Collaboration defined

The difference between a connection and collaboration

How to turn a connection into collaboration

What collaboration produces that you couldn't produce on your own

Collaborative intelligence

Collaborations that made or changed history

How collaborations develop

What collaboration looks like when it works

What to look for in a collaborative relationship

How collaboration creates a win-win

The Four "I"s of Collaboration

The best kind of collaboration partner

To our many friends and colleagues who brought this book to life by generously sharing their knowledge, advice, and stories.

——◄○►——

"The meeting of two personalities is like the contact of two chemical substances: if there is any reaction, both are transformed."

— *Carl Jung*

PRAISE FOR THIS BOOK

W HAT PEOPLE ARE SAYING about *Building Your Business Through Relationships: Contacts, Connections, and Collaboration*

————◄O►————

"If you are a business owner and you read only one chapter of this book and glean only one idea that will help you to move your business forward, it is truly well worth the cost of purchasing!"

- Diane Carson CMC
President, Promo Xpertz LLC
636-399-7777
www.gopromoxpertz.com

"This book helped me realize that contacts are great, but connections are better. The authors lay out a blueprint for turning contacts into connections. It is so much more than just an advice book setting forth theories of how to improve your networking opportunities. It is the 'how-to' book to deepen and build relationships and how to incubate those connections to improve your business, improve your income, and improve your life."

- Debbie S. Champion #38637
  Rynearson Suess Schnurbusch & Champion, LLC
  500 N. Broadway, Suite 1550
  St. Louis, MO 63102
  314-421-4430
  dchampion@rssclaw.com

"Strong business relationships play a critical role in business. In *Building Your Business Through Relationships,* Bobbi Linkemer and Karen Hoffman demonstrate how something as simple as a handshake can lead to opportunities to work together, help one another, and contribute to the larger community. These activities form a solid foundation on which to build any business."

* Maxine Clark
  Founder, Build-A-Bear Workshop
  www.clark-fox.com

"After being in the business world since 1991, I thought I knew a TON about connections and collaboration, but after reading this, I realize how much more I can learn! With their simple steps and strategies, plus advice from others, this 'how-to' book can be used by anyone, from a beginner to an experienced businessperson, to build better business relationships. Buy it today! Buy it for your team!"

* Mason Duchatshek
  mason@buildatribe
  http://www.buildatribe.com

"If you've been stuck in a rut and need fresh ideas about how to build your business through authentic connections, you'll find a wealth of knowledge and practical guidance in this book that will inspire and motivate you to expand your horizons by expanding your circle of connections."

* Nancy Erickson, The Book Professor
  http://www.thebookprofessor.com/

"The power in this book lies in the examples that remind readers of the emotions they feel as they move from contacts through connections to collaboration. For it's in our emotions that we find the energy to act."

- Dale Furtwengler, Author of Lead a Life of CONFI-DENCE and One with the Universe

 314-707-3771

 PricingForProfitBook.com

"If you're in business, you need to network, and you need to have a full understanding of how to nurture that network. I love this book! Karen and Bobbi are experts at building powerful connections that are truly worthy of celebration."

- Mich Hancock, Owner, 100th Monkey Media

 Executive Director, TEDxGatewayArch

 www.100thmm.com

"A business is not built with bricks, hammers, and nails. It is built with a great team of others working together. *Building Your Business Through Relationships: Contacts, Connections, and*

Collaboration, contains the real tools you need to build your business and your dreams."

- Kevin Hocker Award-winning Author, The Success Compass

  Phone: 720-230-7224

  Toll Free: 1-877-317-4167

  Email: Kevin@KevinHocker.com

  www.FedBenefitsGroup.com

  www.TheSuccessCompass.com

"In a world full of possibilities, some people don't see enough, and some people see too many to focus on. This book provides an excellent balance of strategy, tactics, and practical ways to take action, including finding who else can help you."

- Daniel Rubenstein

  www.ALLinEntry.com,

  Daniel@ALLinEntry.com

  314-550-0950

PREFACE

I N THE SUMMER OF 2014, I confessed to my co-author and friend, Bobbi Linkemer, that I did not want to finish the book we had been writing for months. I was concerned that Bobbi might be pretty upset with me for pulling the plug on our project, but when I shared what I felt we REALLY should be writing about, she said, "Thank God! This feels so much more authentic."

I had woken up one morning a few days earlier with this strong desire to help people connect with each other. I felt that Bobbi and I could help them make great connections and find more ways to collaborate. Bobbi understood EXACTLY what my vision was because she is also someone who connects people.

I have devoted my life to being a business resource and connector, but I never realized how much more there was to learn.

Although our book has been out for several years, in the summer of 2020 and COVID, I realized this book needed to be updated. Updated to help us STILL build relationships when life is not easy. Not fair. A little crazy. I approached a dear friend, Shelly Pordea to help Bobbi & I update our book.

We reached out to others in business that have gone through challenging times, not just COVID, but needed to continue building their organizations, hence an updated version of Contacts Connections Collaboration.

Our goal for *Contacts Connections Collaboration* is to go beyond other popular books on our subject by combining elements that are not often found together. On one level, the book is instructional, filled with sound advice. On another level, it is practical because all of the advice in the book has been tried and tested. On yet another level, it is personal, full of Bobbi's and my experiences and feelings and wonderful stories from people we know and respect. Finally, it is sensible, because it is filled with pointers from people who have been there, done that.

It is our hope that this book will become not only a way to grow your business through relationships but also to expand your life by:

- Understanding the significance of making a simple contact and watching where it may lead

- Developing contacts into meaningful connections that have the potential for mutually beneficial relationships

- Turning connections into collaborative relationships in which two or more people work together to achieve a shared mission or goal

• Tips for dealing with life challenges and building/sustaining relationships

This journey only intensified my conviction that Bobbi and I were *supposed to* collaborate on this book about relationships. We wrote what we knew, researched what we didn't know, and reached out to experts in many areas to share their perspectives and advice. While we were passing along their wisdom to our readers, we were also privileged to learn so much from them. Working on this book has become for us a graduate-level course in relationship building.

For Bobbi and me, our relationship has deepened and become a fascinating laboratory for testing our premise. We met years ago (contact), recently explored what we might do together (connection) and worked as a team to create this book (collaboration). In fact, we took it to a fourth level: the magic of synergy.

Adding Shelly Snow Pordea for our updated version, increased our opportunity to collaborate and create synergy. Thank you, Shelly!

We would love to hear from you, our reader. Please visit our Facebook page, Contacts Connections Collaboration.

Positively with love,

Karen

INTRODUCTION

I N AN ARTICLE IN *Forbes*, Mike Muhney, co-inventor of ACT!, a popular contact-management system (CRM), stresses the role relationships play in business: "Relationships determine the job offers you'll get, the consulting contracts you'll win, and the business opportunities you'll be presented with. Yet too many of us don't think strategically about how to cultivate meaningful connections. We just kind of meander along and know we have to make friends and acquaintances, but we don't really think about it."

And now, through the new normal of a global pandemic, or dealing with divergent crises life may throw at us, this book has been updated to help you consciously think about how to cultivate meaningful connections. Contacts and connections will not only aid you during trying times but continue to grow your enterprise when crisis takes a front seat in your life.

Building Through Relationships: Contacts Connections Collaborations and Crisis goes far beyond merely showing you how to use these tools to build your business. It does so by sharing the authors' experiences and passing along advice from experts on almost every subject covered in these pages, tailored specifically to help people facing a tragic circumstance.

There is a logical progression from meeting someone for the first time, whether by intention or by chance, to turning that contact into a deeper connection that leads to collaborating on something you both care about. Ideally, that collaboration generates the powerful state of synergy. The purpose of this book is to guide you through the process and introduce you to many generous professionals who bring the content to life by sharing their expertise and experience with you.

If a picture is indeed better than a thousand words, here is what the step-by-step process looks like.

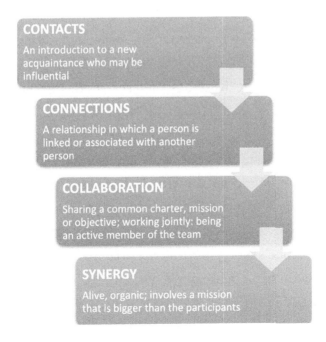

CONTACTS
An introduction to a new acquaintance who may be influential

CONNECTIONS
A relationship in which a person is linked or associated with another person

COLLABORATION
Sharing a common charter, mission or objective; working jointly; being an active member of the team

SYNERGY
Alive, organic; involves a mission that is bigger than the participants

Chapter 1: Contacts

A contact is the first step, an introduction, an exchange of basic information. This chapter covers what you need to know about contacts: what they are; why they're important; where to find them; how to make them; what to do before, during, and after a networking event; and how to establish a system for keeping track and staying in touch with them. In business, especially small business, contacts are currency. They have value. Contacts know things we don't know or people we should meet. A single new contact can lead to something as small as a phone number or as life changing as a new job.

Chapter 2: Connections

A connection is more personal than a contact; it has the potential for a relationship. The chapter explains what connections are, how to establish and sustain them, where they lead, why they are important, and how to become a connector. There are two ways to make connections: by turning a contact into one and by attracting connections in both the face-to-face world and the virtual world. Social media, which puts millions of potential relationships at your fingertips, is discussed extensively in this chapter. While it's tempting to put all of one's energy into this way of connecting, there is still no substitute for getting to know someone in a one-on-one conversation.

Chapter 3: Collaboration

This chapter is about collaboration: what it is, how it grows from connections into something deeper, how to find heart-smart collaboration partners, how to create win-win situations, and why it's important to talk about your goals and dreams with others. If a connection is a way to BE with another person, collaboration is what you and that person DO to achieve something greater than either of you could achieve alone.

Chapter 4: Synergy

Aristotle described synergy as a situation in which "the whole is greater than the sum of its parts" (1 + 1 = 5). There are many other definitions listed at the beginning of this chapter, but frankly, Aristotle's simple explanation has stood the test of time. In collaboration, people work together to achieve a purpose; in synergy, they combine, like chemical elements, to create something new. It is collaboration on steroids. This chapter explains what happens when these chemical elements come together, how they create synergy, and how the combination helps you and others achieve mutual goals.

Chapter 5: Building Through Crises

Examining our world as it has gone through a global pandemic has caused us to reflect on what the principles in this book mean to us when life doesn't go as we expect. In this section, we share stories from people we have interviewed who have gone through unexpected crises like divorce, loss of loved ones, and the aftereffects of Covid-19.

Resources

This section of the book is a perfect example of what happens when you reach out to others to achieve a goal. No two people could have created this book alone. Every contributor who added his or her thoughts and words to *Contacts Connections Collaboration* is listed with their contact information under Resources. In addition, you will find recommended reading and listening materials, business-building organizations, client and database management systems, instructions for how to assemble a get-connected-stay-connected kit, and more.

Memorable quotes

At the end of each chapter are the wise sayings of others that expand the ideas presented here.

In *Future Shock*, futurist Alvin Toffler wrote that change is occurring faster than we can keep up with it. The minute we think we know what something is, it becomes something else. That is certainly true of books. Sometimes, things change before the ink is dry on the page, so be on the lookout for updates. In the meantime, feel free to highlight, add notes, and make it your own.

CONTACTS

T HIS CHAPTER IS ABOUT contacts: what they are; why they're important; where to find them; how to make them; what to do before, during, and after a networking event; and how to establish a system for keeping track of and staying in touch with them. Because we've updated this book after a global shift in the way we live our lives, we want to be sure to emphasize the importance of building relationships even through difficult times. These techniques are great during a "normal" flow of life, but can still be adapted when you are going through challenges.

During crises, you likely won't have the bandwidth to focus on more than a couple of the principles we share. But it's important to note that you are in a different mode of operation. Start by deciding what part of your story–if any–you are ready to share, and how much of yourself you can dedicate to concentrating on engaging with new contacts and collaborating with others. Because, let's face it, probably now more than ever, you need people.

Defining contacts

We are going to parse words here so that we can draw a thin line between contacts, connections, and collaboration, even though we know they tend to blend and overlap a bit. Sometimes, you only recognize the definition you're looking for when you see the ones that don't capture what you want to say. Here are seven ways to define contact. For our purposes, we like the first three best.

1. *Wikipedia*: a person who can offer help in achieving goals

2. *Webster's New World College Dictionary*: The state of being in contact, communication, or association; an acquaintance, especially one who is influential

3. *Dictionary.com*: an acquaintance, colleague, or relative through whom a person can access information, favors, or influential people

4. *Mac Dictionary*: a meeting, communication, or relationship with someone

5. *Merriam-Webster*: an occurrence in which people communicate with each other; the establishment of communication

6. *The Free Dictionary*: a person who might be of use; a connection

7. *Wiktionary*: someone with whom one is in communication

Why contacts are important

Remember John Donne's poem, "No man is an island?" Well, no one in business, especially an entrepreneur, can build a business alone. We all need a little help along the path to success. We need people who know things we don't know or know other people we need to meet. We need contacts. A single new contact can lead to outcomes you never could have imagined—from something as small as a phone number to as life-altering as a new career or even saving a life. Contacts become the links to new opportunities, jobs, clients, business alliances, circumstances, mentors or partners, friends, other new contacts, and deeper connections (see Chapter 2). Contacts introduce you to those who can help you, those who can hire you, and those who can do all the things you can't do or at least don't do well.

Why your credibility matters

Credibility is the quality of being trusted, convincing, and believable. Your credibility becomes apparent to others little by little as they get to know you. Credibility includes several elements, including visual (appropriate image), trustworthiness (discretion, lack of judgment), competence (expertise), and integrity (consistency, transparency).

- **Visual**: People who meet you for the first time make an instant assessment that starts at your face and ends at your feet. That means everything counts, from your hairstyle to your shoes. This is a totally subjective impression, but you do have the power to project exactly the image you want people to see.

- **Trustworthiness**: This is an immediate impression as well, but it is intuitive rather than obvious. Trust is more than knowing that a person will keep your confidences, won't repeat what you say, and won't gossip about you behind your back. The other part of being trustworthy is subtle; it's a sixth sense that you are "safe," that you will be accepted for who you are. It only takes a moment to determine if this is the case or if you should watch what you say.

- **Competence**: How does someone know if you are competent when she first meets you? Your first impression is a judgment that also is made quickly. Do you look the part? Do you speak authoritatively? Do you project your education and experience without reciting your resume? Has she heard of you and, if so, what is your reputation? If someone introduces you, he will probably talk about your qualifications, which will certainly be a good start.

- **Integrity:** This is a rare quality—hard to define, harder to find, but immediately recognizable when it is present. In other words, you know it when you see it and feel it. A person with integrity is honorable and authentic. He has a code of ethics and lives by it, even when it's inconvenient or difficult to do. When he gives his word, you can take it to the bank. Of all the characteristics you would look for in others and want to develop in yourself, integrity is the most valuable.

Karen on visual credibility

"This part is a bit challenging for me, and I feel vulnerable sharing my feelings so openly. Yet, I think it is important to be authentic if we are going be of help to our readers who are trying to make contacts that become connections. After a lifetime of being 'normal weight'—five feet, eight inches and size twelve to fourteen—in 1997, I put on sixty pounds in six months while going through chemotherapy and taking steroids for ovarian cancer. I gained even more weight after that. I saw and felt the difference in the way people perceived me when I first met them. The weight had a negative impact on my career. Someone new, who had just assumed a leadership position in his organization, bluntly told me that I did not project the professional appearance necessary for him to work with me, regardless of the amazing results I had achieved for the organization. So, to be honest, my visual credibility is not that great. However, I am blessed with incredible emotional credibility.

"I really do love people, and they almost always forget that I am a heavy gal. My passion is helping others and making heart-to-heart connections. Most people I meet become my friends. Many adore me and show it in unbelievable ways. I do try to dress professionally, and I credit my image-consultant friends—Nancy Nix-Rice, Donna Gamache, Melissa Lovvorn Steele, and Melody Murray—for their positive effect on my appearance.

"In particular, Nancy has become my go-to person because she has not only felt her clients' pain when they were hard to fit or couldn't find the best colors to wear, she also launched a company called *Components*. She has the colors and the styles she feels are best for me to wear, and when I wear them, I get lots of compliments. Please know that if your appearance isn't picture-perfect, you can still make great connections, as I have been fortunate enough to do. I truly believe that if you have challenges with your visual credibility, as I do, you can overcome them by loving more and judging less."

Bobbi on aging

"Aging is an issue for many of us in a society that really does not value the 'wisdom' of older people, especially women. After a certain point, even in the professional world, women begin to feel invisible, as if we don't even cast a shadow. In my case, it is important to have a professional image that inspires confidence in people who want to hire me.

"What does that take? For one thing, it takes having a robust presence on the Internet. That's how many of my clients find me. My photo, which is recent, does not reveal my age. Somebody asked me if I'm going to 'go gray.' Absolutely not.

When you are in the business world, you don't go gray because you automatically add ten years to your age. It would be lovely if we could be authentic. Authenticity is something I have written about for many years. It is a critical factor in building a solid professional image. But it is very hard to be completely authentic when age is not considered an asset.

"Even though it has taken me close to fifty years to accumulate the knowledge and experience I bring to my clients, one of these days, somebody is going to say to me, 'You are *how* old?' What I've accomplished won't matter; what will matter is how long I've been around. I don't know of a solution for aging. It is inevitable. My approach is to keep on working at what I love for as long as I am fortunate enough to do it.

"I am incredibly proud of the authors I have helped to write and publish their books. The last two authors I worked with were referrals from a satisfied client. That's what we all hope for: great referrals. My website attracts people who seem to feel that I am real. They connect with me as a human being. They want to meet me and talk about their books. My body of work gives me a lot of credibility. And I put 110 percent of effort into every job I do. So far, that's working, and so am I."

How to find contacts

They are all around you, everywhere you go. Really, all it takes is an introduction. You introduce yourself, the other person introduces herself, or someone introduces you to each other. You chat for a while. You exchange pertinent information and business cards. You shake hands and go your separate ways, but if you understand the value and potential of that brief encounter, you keep that person's business card and follow up. (More about that later.)

When you're going through a difficult time, you may not have the opportunity to do many of the things listed below. But if you focus on ONE per week (or choose a timespan that is feasible to your crisis schedule) whether virtual or in person, your connections can continue to grow. Some places are natural hangouts for potential contacts; others take a little more effort. Here are some excellent places to start:

- **Alumni groups** (high school, college, sororities or fraternities, academic honor societies) – People you knew way back when are like hidden treasures in terms of contacts. Not only are they valuable in their own right but also in terms of *their* contacts. They have lived a whole lifetime since you last saw them, and you have no idea what they've been up to. A quick email may be all it takes to reconnect.

- **College/high school reunions** – Maybe you haven't seen some of these people in years and can barely put a name with a face. But then you get into a casual conversation and discover that you have more in common with this person now than you did when you went to school together. How could you have known what career path he would choose or who he knows whom you should know as well?

- **Chambers of commerce** (local, statewide, regional)

– If you do business in your neighborhood or city, local chambers of commerce are the best places to meet potential customers, clients, and barter partners. If you have time, get involved with local business organizations, and turn those contacts into mutually beneficial connections. In order to maximize your chamber experience, find a group or committee that interests you, and volunteer to work on it.

- **Chance encounters** – You run into an old friend or business colleague when you least expect it. If you just say, "It's so nice to see you again," and just go on your way, you are missing a great opportunity. Here is a contact right in front of you, so unless you are late for an appointment, stop for a moment, chat, and exchange business cards. You never know where it will lead.

- **Conventions, conferences** – These planned events, no matter what their purpose, are designed for making contacts. If you don't collect a pile of business cards and scribble pertinent information on them, you have missed half of what you came here to do—make contacts and connections. Not only are there people everywhere, they are interested in the same things you are. In a sense, they are self-qualified.

- **Exercise and fitness facilities** – Let's face it, it's not easy to meet someone on the next treadmill or recumbent but there are ways to start a conversation in the weight room, the locker room, or a classroom. People do make friends in fitness and yoga classes, and you never know when one of your fellow Pilates or Zumba buddies will turn into a business contact as well.

- **Facebook events and LinkedIn special-interest groups** – Like conferences, special-interest groups on social media sites are made to order for meeting like-minded people. Whatever you are into, there is a group dedicated to that subject. In fact, you will probably be overwhelmed with choices in your field. While it's tempting to join all of them, do a little research first. Chances are you won't be able to participate in more than a few, and active participation is what these groups are all about. So, pick one or two that really interest you, check in frequently, and *participate*. That could mean answering questions, posing questions, or sharing information.

- **Introductions** – These are powerful, and Karen is a master at introducing people who she feels should meet each other. Her introductions have a strategic business purpose; people value them and follow up; and they frequently lead to surprising outcomes. Introductions are so easy. If you know two people who have the potential to help each other, drop them an email that says, "You two ought to meet," and explain why. Then, stand back, and watch the magic happen.

- **Meetup groups** – What social media groups accomplish online, meetups do off-line. Meetup.com is the place to find and join groups dedicated to subjects of interest to you, such as politics, books, business, specific industries, health, marketing, or hobbies. Their benefits include learning more about your favorite subject and, of course, making new and valuable face-to-face contacts.

- **Neighborhood, condo, or homeowners' associations** – The people you meet at organizations centered around where you live share a collective goal: to take care of the neighborhood in order to maintain property values. While your neighbors may have a similar socioeconomic status, they may come from different backgrounds, have different careers, and bring different ideas to the group. Not only will they broaden your perspectives, it is possible they can help you in some way, such as finding a handyman, babysitter, or doctor close to home.

- **Networking events** – These provide wonderful opportunities to meet new people and exchange fundamental facts about your businesses. For extroverts, they are just big parties; for introverts, they can be more of a challenge. There are two keys to successfully negotiating networking events: (1) Treat them as tactics in your overall marketing plan, not as dreaded, obligatory affairs you'd rather skip; and (2) think of them as research opportunities. Put the spotlight on the *other* person; become a good interviewer; ask questions; listen more, talk less.

- **Newspaper/magazine calendar events** – Where do you find the right networking events to attend? One of the best places to look is in the calendar section of the daily newspaper, your city's magazine, or an industry newsletter or website. If you are a natural networker, you already know this and have probably made it a habit to check for events that you'd like to attend. But if you're new at this or perhaps a little hesitant to attend an event full of strangers, this is going to take some determination and discipline. Unless you are a bona fide extrovert, you may need a little help. Keep reading.

- **Places of worship** – If you are looking for people on your spiritual wavelength, one of the best places to find them is at your church, temple or synagogue, mosque, or community meeting room. At the very least, you will have one shared interest. That is all it takes to make your first contact. From that point, a few simple questions will tell you if you have even more in common.

- **Professional/trade associations** – From a business standpoint, you can't do much better than a whole group of people who are interested in what you do for a living or are connected to your business in some way. Every person you talk to is an automatic contact. While you could probably talk shop for hours, you may find yourselves wandering off the topic and exploring other avenues. If you have one thing in common, chances are you have more. Just remember to talk to other people. Try not to monopolize one person but to bring others into the conversation, which will expand your circle instantly.

- **Research librarian at your local library** – For writers, authors, and researchers, the research department of the public library is still the best place to hang out, and the librarian is their number one contact. But research librarians will help anyone, even non-writers, and you should have at least one such expert on your contact list. With a few well-placed keystrokes, a research librarian can connect you to the world. And in case you still prefer to comb through voluminous books, she has them at her fingertips. Research librarians can also help with demographic or geographic databases, as well as find the best associations for you, all at no cost.

- **Social events** (charities, auctions, dinners, and cocktail parties) – Just because you're all dressed up and having fun doesn't mean you leave your relationship hat at home. New acquaintances and old friends who attend the same functions you do are potential contacts you may never have considered. Small talk doesn't have to be superficial; it can (and should) be focused on getting to know more about other people. Come to think of it, that's the definition of making contacts.

- **Social media sites and groups** – If your first thoughts are Facebook and LinkedIn, that's great, but don't stop there. There are many less well-known sites you might want to investigate. If everybody and his brother are on Facebook, why not try Google+ (Guy Kawasaki wrote a whole book about it called *What the Plus! Google+ for the Rest of Us),* Tumblr, Instagram, Flickr, Vine, or Stumbleupon? Go even deeper into social networking, and discover Quora, About.me, Keek, Crowdtilt, Delicious, Foursquare, and Slideshare. And there are dozens more!

What to do before a networking event

Any time you go to an event, you are making an investment of your time, your energy, and/or your money. So, if you're planning to go, leverage your investment by thinking through what you want and being prepared. You wouldn't go camping or on a trip without getting ready. This is no different except that a networking event can pay big dividends in terms of new relationships, new business, new clients, and maybe even new friends. What follows are some ways to proactively prepare to take advantage of networking opportunities:

- Block out time on your calendar to add new contacts' business cards as soon as possible after the event. If you can do this within twenty-four to seventy-two hours, you will still be fresh in people's minds. It is especially important to set aside more time for this activity when you attend large events or conferences.

- Create a template letter you can use, modify, or personalize for the follow-up email after events you attend.

- Have a reason to attend this particular event. "The *real* goal of attending a networking event should be to connect with people you can either help or do business with," advises **Donna Gamache**, a friend of Karen's who used to run networking groups. "Network with the end results in mind. If possible, check out the guest list, and have a plan for whom you want to meet and get to know."

- Communicate in advance with the president, membership chair, or program chair to say that you will be attending. Then, ask:

- How can I leverage my time and energy?

- What contribution might I make to the group?

- Who are some of the people I should make time to

connect with first? (Karen loved this tip from *The 7 Levels of Communication* by Michael Maher.)

- This is pretty basic: Know *where you're going and how to get there*; allow plenty of time to arrive earlier than you need to. Starting off late or getting lost can affect your ability to be relaxed and ready to connect. By showing up early, you will have time to stop in the restroom to check your appearance and, of course, to increase your chances of meeting people. If the event is being held at a hotel, allow time for parking and finding the room. If you have paid to go to this event and you arrive late, you may forgo some great opportunities to mingle and make strategic connections. If there is a speaker, you don't want to miss any of his talk or interrupt him in mid-presentation. One more point: You never know how you could be of help to someone else, but if you are late, you lower your chances of finding out.

- Before you get out of your car, take a minute to *check your positivity quotient*—how optimistic, enthusiastic, and upbeat do you feel? If your self-assessment says "not much," you need an instant attitude adjustment. Take a deep breath and smile. (No one can see you; you're in your car.) Check your smile in your pull-down mirror. Now, try to keep that pleasant expression as you head to the event.

- For a more scientific approach, take this happiness

quiz (http://tinyurl.com/pchd6zb) and see how you rate. If your quotient isn't as high as you would like it to be, take a moment to readjust your thinking. After all, who would *you* prefer to talk to—someone who is complaining about the weather or the traffic or the food or, worse yet, other people, or someone who is cheerful and pleasant? If you feel that way, it's safe to assume others do, too.

- Center yourself in whatever way works for you: Meditate for a moment. Do a quick-and-easy relaxation exercise. Take a few deep breaths, and stand up straight. Say a short prayer. Ask for help from a higher power. Visualize yourself being cheerful, open, calm. Anticipate meeting great people, making valuable contacts, having fun, and helping others.

- Be honest with yourself about your personality. Are you an introvert? If so, remember that people love to talk about themselves, so all you have to do is ask questions to get the conversation going. On the other hand, if you are an extrovert, questions work here as well. Getting other people talking is a good way to keep yourself from dominating the conversation. As an added benefit, you might learn something.

- Create a be-connected, stay-connected system—a small plastic storage container with a locking lid, which will contain everything you might need at any event and help you follow up after the event. In it, put

your business cards, QR code (quick response code
that can be read by a cell phone), pens or pencils,
snack-sizeZiploc bags, 3x5-inch index cards, mini
Post-it® notes, and a mini stapler. (See Resources.)

- Keep track of your contacts. You could use something
  as simple as Microsoft Outlook or an Excel spreadsheet, or consider a customer relationship management system (CRM), like ACT!, Insightly, or Hatchbuck. There are lots of choices. Here's how to find
  them: Do a search on Google, Bing, Yahoo, or your
  favorite search engine, and ask your business associates for referrals. Social media sites are another good
  way to keep in touch with people and build your network (e.g., Facebook personal or business page, Facebook groups, LinkedIn groups, or some of the less
  well-known but powerful sites). For a more complete
  list, see Resources.

- Find someone to help you create and maintain your
  database. Unless you love doing data entry, hire
  someone who can help you keep your contacts up to
  date. Check out Craigslist; ask a family member or a
  neighbor; find an intern at one of the local colleges
  or universities; or hire a virtual assistant (VA) Check
  here for one source. https://www.freelancer.com/fin
  d/Virtual-Assistant/ This is an important marketing
  investment in your "relationship management" system.

- **Lori Feldman**, known as The Database Diva, feels that it's all about the list. "The biggest mistake people make," says Lori, "is not building a contact list." The way she builds hers is by focusing more on *getting* business cards than on giving people hers; she doesn't even take business cards to events. When people ask if she has a card, she says, "No, but give me yours, and I'll send you all my information." That way, she is building her own contact list.

To stay connected, it is absolutely imperative to have a database or CRM program to track contact information, notes, and activities. For many years Karen used ACT! software for her database management until Lori Feldman introduced her to Hatchbuck, a sales and marketing system that includes CRM, email marketing, and marketing automation—a pretty comprehensive system! Bobbi is still searching for the perfect (very simple) system.

- **Don Breckenridge**, the founder of Hatchbuck, which was sold to Benchmark One is a problem solver and "geek" with a history of software development. In the late nineties, one of his largest clients in his custom-software-development firm no longer needed his services. Don had an idea about developing recruiting software. Coincidentally, Don's client had been a recruiter and understood the software concept. He offered to invest in the idea. So, Don and his new partner began their profitable collaboration by creating Sendouts, a company that helped thousands of recruiters around the world find the right candidates for available positions.

Sendouts, which was purchased by another company, used marketing automation to grow its customer base, but marketing automation was expensive and highly technical. Small businesses have trouble staying in touch with customers, let alone prospects. Don wanted to create a less expensive program that combined database management, CRM, email marketing, and automation to help smaller companies run their companies more efficiently, all at a price point they could afford.

And thus, Hatchbuck, now Benchmark One, was born. Its purposes were to help businesses stay organized, nurture prospects and customers, and identify contacts who were most sales-ready.

One of their strengths is that they identify contacts who are opening emails, clicking on links, visiting a website, and even the pages they click on. It is much more efficient to reach out to a specific contact who is connecting back to your business than random contacts or your whole database. With Hatchbuck, relationships can be built through automated marketing. Building and maintaining relationships seems easier with Hatchbuck than with ACT! and other CRMs, and the price point for all that Hatchbuck offers is more affordable than using several systems to accomplish various tasks.

As a side note, when Karen met with Don to discuss Hatchbuck for our book, she learned that he has a nonprofit background as well, moving him from a contact to a connection.

When Don visited the Gateway to Dreams website, he shared ideas for other initiatives that could possibly lead to a mutually beneficial collaboration. This is a perfect example about how a contact can lead to a connection that, ideally, will become a collaboration.

- **Sarah Petty** is a gifted photographer, a partner in Joy of Marketing (www.JoyofMarketing.com) and author of *Worth Every Penny*. She is a great believer in the value of databases. "Everyone in business should have one, and everyone you know should be in it," she says. "All of your clients, the media, your friends, and your family. It doesn't have to be a fancy CRM program. We have our own program that allows us to write personal notes.

"This is a high-touch, Web-based program because we want to be able to pull up people's pages as we are talking to them. We tag each entry in one or more of our twelve categories and market to different categories differently. VIP clients go in a separate category. We all want more customers or clients. If we just go back to our databases, it's so much easier than starting from scratch. Sarah's advice: "Build your database slowly and gradually. Don't wait until you need it."

Sarah Petty's database categories:

- Clients, business associates (everyone she does business with)

- Co-marketing partners (people with whom she wants to partner, whether or not she knows them)

- Friends & family (need to be kept in the loop)

- Mistakes (gives extra love to anyone in this category)

- Spouse's contacts (will receive a holiday card)

- Prospects (anyone who responds to her marketing)

- Temp (prospects who she emails once or twice, hoping to get a response)

- VIP clients (more valuable)

- Media (*must* establish relationships with the media)

- Fellow photographers (people in her industry)

- Marketing students (high school and college kids whom she mentors)

- Other smaller, miscellaneous groups to which she belongs

Like Sarah Petty, Karen has added many categories to her database management program, in order to let her contacts know about events or make connections. Some are business-related; some are more personal, such as:

- Animal lovers

- Speakers

- Coaches

- Authors

- Spiritual communities

Something else to keep in mind is that, when you get ready to sell your business, a large, well-maintained, and active database can add to the value of your company.

What to do *during* a networking event

OK. You're in the door. You're prepared. It's time to network, which simply means meet people or, as Karen likes to say, "build relationships." You look around and see a sea of faces. Here are some ways to negotiate the crowd.

Start with a smile—a real one. "Being genuine and yourself helps you feel confident," says **Donna Gamache**. "People are naturally attracted to that. If you don't know anyone there, start a conversation about a neutral subject. Then, ask one or two questions about the other person. Questions are powerful icebreakers. They help you find things in common. The key is to wait until you are asked before you share any information about yourself."

- **Mary Kuthies**, founder of MCK Coaching: Get Focused. Accomplish More, is a consummate networker. Her advice in a nutshell is, "In any networking situation, you can't fail if you follow these Three Rules for Building Relationships: Ask more than tell; listen more than talk; be more concerned about being interest*ed* than interest*ing*.

"Too often at networking events," Mary observes, "it seems as though there is a secret contest for who can collect the most business cards. While intentions may be good, when folks get back to their busy offices, the cards get tossed in an ever-growing pile on the desk—the black hole of undeveloped connections.

"What *should* be happening," she says, "is that you take the cards, and you follow up on each one with an email, call, or note. You add them to your contact list. Maybe they add themselves to your subscriber list. You make a connection on LinkedIn or perhaps Facebook, if that's your thing. You schedule lunch or coffee in order to begin developing a true business relationship."

It only takes a few seconds to exchange business cards, but it takes a lot more time to follow up on the ones you've collected. "You've only got so much time in a day," Mary points out. "So go for quality relationships, not quantity of cards."

The best way to develop "quality relationships," advises international best-selling author and speaker **Bob Burg,** is to shift your emphasis. "The successful networkers I know," says Burg, "continually put the other person's needs ahead of their own."

A surprising number of people who attend networking events are introverts, for whom this is not always a favorite activity. **Cathy Sexton,** a productivity expert and self-proclaimed introvert, tries to limit the number of people she talks to at such get-togethers. "For an introvert," she says, "sometimes, it's better to meet one or two people, go deep, and get to know them better. It also helps to go to the event with someone you know—to create a safety anchor. Come in together," she suggests. "First, split up and meet people; then, come together again. That way, you always know someone there."

It sometimes helps to know who is going to be at the event and at least have your first conversation with someone you have met in the past. If there is a published list, try to find out who's attending. Meetup publishes its list of attendees for each event. If you don't particularly relish walking into a room full of strangers, having a list ahead of time may alleviate some of your discomfort.

- **Will Hanke** is a Web and SEO expert. He suggests that if, on the other hand, you are an extrovert, you can help others feel more at ease. You might want to help with registration at the table or stand near the table to welcome people informally. Befriend someone who looks uncomfortable. Start by sharing some basic information—your name, why you are at this particular event, what you do for a living. Then, ask a few neutral questions. These are icebreakers that lead to more in-depth conversations. If your city is as tight as St. Louis, Missouri, you will discover that you have at least a few mutual friends or associates. The rule of thumb is to keep the conversation positive and upbeat, even if the best thing you can think of to compliment are the table settings and selection of hors d'oeuvres.

If you do collect business cards, be sure to make notes about each person you meet on the back of her business card or on a sticky note. Jot down more details on a 3x5 card, in a small notebook, on your smart phone, in Notes, or in Evernote.

- **Bob Baker,** who helps musicians, writers, artists, and creative entrepreneurs use their talents and know-how to make a living and make a difference in the world, admits that he probably could be more strategic at networking events. "I usually go into them with the attitude that I'm going to meet cool new people and make some new friends," he says. "So I don't put too much pressure on myself to generate X number of leads or meet certain types of people. However, there is a time and place to target people who are in a position to help your cause. If you can casually meet them at an event, it paves the way for you to follow up and invite them to coffee or lunch."

Sometimes, it's easier to remember what you *shouldn't* do than what you should do. First, think about what networking means: interacting with other people to exchange information and develop contacts, especially to further one's career. It is not an opportunity to deliver a litany of your skills, sell yourself or your company, or broadcast your message. Even though your ultimate goal may be to further your career, the only rule you have to remember is this: When you meet someone at a networking event, *it is not about you; it is about the other person.*

- **Bob Baker's** easy-to-remember list of don'ts:

- Don't talk only about yourself.

- Don't launch right into a pitch about your latest project.

- Don't sell.

- Don't monopolize someone's time at a gathering.

How Karen learned to love networking events

Believe it or not, Karen used to dread going to networking events. It took everything she had to force herself to attend. On her way to one particular event at the former St. Louis Regional Chamber Association (RCGA), she was distraught because her family was at home, and she was about to go somewhere she didn't want to go. She spent an extra-long time in the restroom because she did not want to see all those people she didn't know. Finally, she forced herself to come out and go into the room.

The first people she ran into were Joe Eisenberg, a client, and his then wife, Jamie; Joe introduced her to someone else; then, another person joined the conversation; and pretty soon, they had a crowd. Karen found herself having a good time and changed her attitude completely.

She stopped thinking of networking events as something she dreaded and began to view them as business parties. "I got to know Joe, who was my client, and his wife on a more personal level, and I met many other interesting people. Since then," Karen says, "I have come to see networking events as opportunities to create new friends, even if I know no one when I walk in the door."

What changed for Karen was her perspective: These occasions became opportunities to meet new people (contacts), form new relationships (connections), and share possible life-changing experiences (collaboration).

How Bobbi applied what she learned at college frat parties to the world of business networking

The whole idea of fraternity-sorority exchanges—contrary to what one might think —didn't seem to have anything to do with meeting boys or getting dates. Rather, it was more about sticking close to your sorority sisters and staying safe. Bobbi must have been absent the day they explained those rules because her approach was downright subversive. She would take a deep breath and walk in a straight line until she ran into a guy. Then, she would say, "Hi! My name is Bobbi. What's yours?" It worked every time. The ice was broken and a conversation had begun. Compared to a room full of strange boys and disapproving sorority sisters, networking events are a piece of cake.

How to find areas of common interest

Finding a topic you share with another person can break down even the strongest barriers. There is a story told about the historic meeting at Camp David between Egyptian President Anwar Sadat and Israeli Prime Minister Menachem Begin. Things were not going well, and the talks were stalled when the two men found themselves alone with each other. It was then that they began to share stores of their time spent in prison and of their families and grandchildren. Finally, after thirteen days of wrangling, they had found common ground. It was a beginning. A spark ignited, and they had a connection.

No matter how intimidating you may find the idea of starting a conversation with a total stranger, just remember the power of finding *even one* shared experience to break the ice. For men, the most natural and neutral jump starter is usually sports. It's just a matter of finding the right one among football, baseball, golf, tennis, bowling, racecars, and more. If you find outdoor activities more your style, bring up fishing, hunting, horseback riding, white-water rafting, or skiing.

Geography is an almost foolproof starting point. Just ask someone, Where do you live? or Where did you grow up? In our hometown, St. Louis, the question everyone asks is, Where did you go to high school? (Karen went to McCluer. Bobbi is not a native St. Louisan, so she usually makes up a school. It gets the conversation rolling, especially if she has to admit she really went to high school in Chicago.) Karen believes the high school question is a way of helping people connect through mutual acquaintances, landmarks, activities, and neighborhoods.

TV shows everyone is watching, the latest great movie, or the book you can't put down usually work, as does the subject of pets—any pet, from a new puppy to some exotic species to no pets and why you are living such a deprived life. The secret is simply to pick something that interests *you*, and you may find it also interests the person you've just met. Short of quantum mechanics (and sometimes, even that), almost any topic will generate some interest and response.

What to do after a networking event

Time really does fly when you're having fun, so if you enjoyed yourself, chances are this party will be over before you know it. You leave with your be-connected, stay-connected system loaded with business cards and scribbled notes and the de-termination to follow up on every one of them. Here is where the real contact collectors really shine. You have a system; here's how it works.

- The first thing you do, immediately after the event, is use social media to reach out to those with whom you have made the strongest connection. Do it while you are still fresh in each other's minds. If you are not al-ready friends, contacts, or followers, send a personal invitation with a quick reminder of where and when you met.

- Next, enter contacts and notes in your database or client-management system. Jot down where you met, who introduced you, what you talked about, or hand over this important task over to someone else. (See Resources.) All the notes you add can help jog your memory as you meet and add even more people to your database. Karen swears by her notes to remind her where and when she met a contact so that she can remember them on a deeper level. And you truly never know when you might experience a reconnection that can make a huge difference in your life.

- Reach out with an email to each new contact (this is important), follow up on anything you promised to do, and send anything you offered to send (information, an introduction). Do it now; don't wait.

- Find ways to stay in touch. Send helpful articles, make introductions, suggest upcoming events, pass along links to relevant websites and blogs.

Karen was a regular reader of a weekly column in the *St. Louis Post Dispatch* written by Tim McGuire. It was called "More Than Work." She wrote Tim to express her appreciation for his stories and told him about local companies and people who subscribed to his heartfelt business philosophies. Tim and Karen became email friends, and Karen suggested more people Tim might want to interview.

Tim followed up with a phone call to ask about the people Karen had mentioned in her emails. In the course of their conversation, he decided he wanted to interview Karen. His story was about the synchronistic event that followed her emotional breakdown while she was driving alone in her car. The story went national and allowed Karen to connect with new people and reconnect with those she had known in the past. This all started with an email to acknowledge Tim for his great column and is a perfect example of never knowing where a simple act will lead.

Conclusion

Contacts are acquaintances, especially those who have influence and can help you achieve your goals. They are important because they can become the links to new opportunities, jobs, clients, business alliances, circumstances, mentors or partners, other new contacts, and deeper connections. Contacts are the first step on a staircase that leads to lasting, productive relationships and outcomes beyond anything you may have imagined. They are important because they can become the links to new opportunities, jobs, clients, business alliances, circumstances, mentors or partners, other new contacts, and deeper connections. Contacts are the first step on a staircase that leads to lasting, productive relationships and outcomes beyond anything you may have imagined.

MEMORABLE QUOTES

"WE WANT TO REINVENT the phone. What's the killer app? The killer app is making calls! It's amazing how hard it is to make calls on most phones. We want to let you use contacts like never before." —*Steve Jobs*

"Sometimes you have to disconnect to stay connected. Remember the old days when you had eye contact during a conversation? When everyone wasn't looking down at a device in their hands? We've become so focused on that tiny screen that we forget the big picture, the people right in front of us." —*Regina Brett*

"During the past few decades, modern technology, with radio, TV, air travel, and satellites, has woven a network of communication which puts each part of the world into almost instant contact with all the other parts." —*David Bohm*

"There are four ways, and only four ways, in which we have contact with the world. We are evaluated and classified by these four contacts: what we do, how we look, what we say, and how we say it." —*Dale Carnegie*

"It is not what we learn in conversation that enriches us. It is the elation that comes of swift contact with tingling currents of thought." —*Agnes Repplier*

"The worst mistake of first contact, made throughout history by individuals on both sides of every new encounter, has been the unfortunate habit of making assumptions. It often proved fatal." —*David Brin*

"Basic human contact—the meeting of eyes, the exchanging of words—is to the psyche what oxygen is to the brain. If you're feeling abandoned by the world, interact with anyone you can." —*Martha Beck*

"I have a big thing with eye contact, because I think as soon as you make eye contact with somebody, you see them, and they become valued and worthy." —*Mary Lambert*

QUICK REMINDERS

Places to find contacts

Educational	Business	Internet-based
• Alumni groups • College and high school re-unions	• Chambers of com-merce • Conventions & conferences • Professional or trade associations	• Facebook/ LinkedIn Special-Interest Groups • Meetups • Other social media sites & groups
Social	**Public/Other**	**Other Re-sources**
• Introductions • Meetups • Neighborhood, condo, and home-owners associations • Networking events • Places of wor-ship • Social events	• Chance encounters • Exercise and fit-ness facilities	• Newspapers • Magazines • Online calendars

---

What to Do Before an Event

Why this event?

Do you have a reason to attend this particular event?

What is it?

Do you know anyone who will be there?

How can you find out?

Whom would you like to meet?

If you attend the event, to whom should you reach out?

Can you talk to someone in advance to say you will be attending and ask (blank)?

- How can you can get the most out of this event?

- What contribution might you make to the group?

- Who should you connect with first?

- President's name and contact information

Membership chair's name and contact information

Program chair's name and contact information

Who is the speaker?

What's the subject of the talk?

Why does this interest you?

On a scale of 1 to 10, how optimistic, enthusiastic, and up-beat are you about this event?

On a scale of 1 to 10, how much do you anticipate meeting great people, making valuable contacts, and having fun?

Logistics

Where is the event being held? What is the address?

Do you know how to get there/use your GPS?

What time should you be there?

What time do you have to leave to make it on time?

Where will you park?

If the event is in a hotel, where is the room?

Immediately *before* the event

How will you center yourself?

___ Meditate for a moment

___ Do a quick-and-easy relaxation exercise

___ Take a few deep breaths

___ Say a short prayer

___ Ask for help from a higher power

___ Visualize yourself being cheerful, open, calm

At the event

What are the first few questions you will ask someone you don't know?

1. _____

2. _____

3. _____

Do you have a be-connected, stay-connected system? (Travel Kit for your car?)

___ Small plastic storage container with a locking lid

___ Your business cards

___ QR code & QR code scanner on your smartphone

___ Pens or pencils

___ Snack-size Ziploc bags

___ 3X5-inch index cards

___ Mini Post-it® notes

___ Mini stapler

After the event to follow up

Do you have a system for keeping track of your contacts?

___ Microsoft Outlook

___ Excel spreadsheet

___ Customer relationship management system (CRM)

___ Social media

Do you have someone to help you maintain your database?
If so, whom?

If not, have you checked:

___ Craigslist

___ Family member, friend, or neighbor

___ Intern at one of the local colleges or universities

___ Virtual assistant (VA)

＊＊＊

What to Do After an Event

Now, you are ready to become a super connector.

- Sort your business cards; put the ones with whom you have made the strongest connection on the top of the pile.

- Look at any notes you have written.

- Reach out on Facebook, LinkedIn, Twitter, and other social media sites.

- If you are not already friends, contacts, or followers, send a personal invitation with a quick reminder of where and when you met.

- Enter contacts and notes in your database or client-management system. Jot down where you met, who introduced you, and what you talked about.

- Reach out with an email to each new contact.

- Follow up on anything you promised to do.

- Send anything you offered to send (information, an introduction, etc.).

- Find ways to stay in touch.

- Send helpful articles.

- Make introductions.

- Suggest upcoming events.

CONNECTIONS

"Connection is the energy that is created between people when they feel seen, heard, and valued; when they can give and receive without judgment."

—Brené Brown

THIS CHAPTER IS ABOUT connections: what they are, how to establish and sustain them, where they lead, why they're important, and how to become a connector.

Defining connections

A connection is a relationship in which a person is linked or associated with another person.

The difference between a contact and a connection

- A contact is the first step, an introduction, an exchange of basic information (name, profession,

- company); it may be casual, surface knowledge, not even be face to face.

- A connection, on the other hand, is more personal and in-depth, and with the potential for a relationship.

- How it feels: A contact could be pleasant and fun. It's kind of a "Hi, how are you?" If I see him again, that's fine; if I don't, that's fine, too. A connection is someone I would want to see again. A connection is someone I will grow to care about. A connection is deeper.

- When people feel seen, heard, and valued, a spark of interest may develop.

- The beginning of a friendship—the fact that two people out of the thousands around them can meet and connect and become friends—seems like a kind of magic. But maintaining a friendship requires work on the part of both people.

How to turn contacts into connections

Karen has a one-word definition: CARE. Care about their lives; care about their kids; care about their careers; care about whatever they care about. Take the risk of getting involved emotionally. When you care, you can't be distant or separate. What does that word mean? Those who care for others are:

C - concerned, compassionate, considerate

A - active listeners, authentic, attentive, appreciative

R - relationship-oriented, real, respectful

E - empathetic, encouraging, engaged

- **Jeffrey Gitomer**—an American author; professional speaker; business trainer; and expert on sales, customer loyalty, and personal development—says, "If you have matching passions or can in other ways make a link with another person, the connection goes from casual to personal." To us, that means from contact to connection.

For many people, it's important to actually get together with people as a way to follow up on that first contact. Karen admits that she doesn't do as much of that as she used to. Over the years, she has built hundreds and hundreds of connections. Bobbi thinks it's the best way to get to know someone better, but it takes determination to make that call, hold that date (even if it's just for coffee), and set aside the time to meet. Once you're sitting across the table from someone, the most amazing things can happen. "People are opportunities," says **Colleen Seifert**, author and professor at the University of Michigan. "The gift is in the interaction and the connection with another person, whether it lasts forever or not."

How to attract new connections in the face-to-face world

- **Be approachable.** It's hard for most people to walk up to a total stranger and start a conversation, but if your presence is an open invitation to take the risk and say "Hi," you will not only make it easy, you might even make it irresistible.

- **Scott Ginsberg** has brought new meaning to these words by wearing a nametag twenty-four/seven for years. The author of *HELLO my name is Scott* and *The Power of Approachability*, he has parlayed a simple idea into a way of life. His website, blog, podcasts, and speaking engagements all focus on one concept: how to be friendly and easy to talk to. Here are three of his suggestions:

"Don't try to be different. In fact, don't try to be anything. Be yourself. Be the world's expert on you, and be that person every day. Nothing is more approachable than authenticity.

"Make it easy for people who come to your website to get in touch with you. On every page, put phone numbers, email, fax, screen names, your mailing address, and any other medium through which customers can reach you.

"Put a mirror by your phone. Every time you answer it, you'll catch a glimpse of yourself and either smile or laugh. And customers (or whoever is on the other end of your conversation) will hear your smile come through the line when you answer."

- **Keep your mind open.** Try not to judge. We don't know when we first meet someone what we might have in common or what is going on in that person's life. "We can all be judgmental," observes **Beth Thater-Maune,** a healer and teacher. "But most people really do try to see others in their best light. Sometimes, we judge people without even knowing we are doing it. We see someone, and based on her actions and appearance, we make a decision about her. To build a bridge to better communication and understanding," says Beth, "you must take the time to understand people and their circumstances and to listen without your own interpretation."

- **Be of service.** If you're being helpful, it seems to open the door for more and deeper connections, more rapport, and untold possibilities. If you have an idea, information, or an introduction that might help someone, pass it along.

"Your income is determined by how many people you serve and how you well serve them," insists **Bob Burg**, co-author of The Go-Giver: *A Little Story About a Powerful Business Idea.* "Shifting your focus from getting to giving is not only a nice way to live and conduct business but a very profitable way as well."

In 2008, The Go-Giver by **Bob Burg** and **John David Mann** hit the shelves for the first time and took the business world by storm. Its message—that shifting our focus from *getting* to giving is the simplest, most fulfilling and most effective path to success in business and in life—has been translated into twenty-four languages and sparked a global movement.

- **Bob Burg** is a highly sought-after speaker who teaches the principles at the core of the *Go Giver* to audiences around the world. He is also the author of *Endless Referrals*. **John David Mann** is the author of *The Zen of MLM: Legacy, Leadership and the Network Marketing Experience* and co-author of *You Call The Shots: Succeed Your Way—and Live the Life You Want* and *A Deadly Misunderstanding: A Congressman's Quest to Bridge the Muslim-Christian Divide.*

- **Arlen Chaleff** is an active listener and a candid talker. She is passionate about the causes she believes in. A diagnosis of bipolar disorder forty years ago turned her life upside down. She had been on an exciting career path with a major data-processing corporation, feeling that the best was yet to come. "I didn't know then that the worst was yet to come," she recalls, "and had no idea how I would have to redefine myself so I could find myself again.

"I lived as best I could between the highs and lows of my illness. I couldn't hold a job, but I found a new way to contribute, to bring back my self-esteem that was so shattered by my illness.

"I became a founding member of a program called WINGS that would provide support and services for individuals living with mental illness and their families. It was under the umbrella of a family and children's services agency, and it survived on a wing and a prayer. We needed a fundraiser, and I made it happen by calling on those in my network.

"Most of them knew me and the challenges I had faced with my illness. This fundraiser for WINGS allowed me to see the success I would have by extending my reach. The event raised enough money to fund our program for a year, and we did it without a budget and with the help of pro bono services."

From WINGS, Arlen moved to another nonprofit agency, National Alliance on Mental Illness (NAMI), an organization founded by families living with mental illness. "I became the first president of the board who had personally lived with mental illness. I brought in old and new connections and gave them the opportunity to serve an agency that critically needed their support and help."

Three years ago, Arlen took her community outreach connections to another nonprofit, HateBrakers, whose mission it is to interrupt the hate-breeds-hate cycle. HateBrakers honors those who have been victims of bullying, abuse, anti-Semitism, racism, genocide, the Holocaust, or other forms of hatred.

"HateBrakers has given me the opportunity to take my connections to another level," says Arlen. "One of our HateBrakers heroes went on to give a keynote address at the graduation of a school for children with challenges. This year, we honored a woman who is helping kids in the Ferguson, Missouri, area find a safe and civil environment to in which to express their feelings and discuss ways to move on from the trauma."

- **Marcia Layton Turner** is a prolific writer and a consummate networker. She has written fourteen business and consumer books; appeared in more than twenty-five consumer, business, and trade magazines; held several marketing and marketing-communications positions; consulted with major national organizations; and launched her own national association.

In 2008, Marcia was at an American Society of Journalists and Authors (ASJA) conference, when someone asked if there was an association for ghostwriters. "The answer was no," she recalls. Two years later, she launched the Association of Ghostwriters. "At the beginning, the goal was to bring together people who were interested in ghostwriting, learning more about it, networking, sharing leads, and helping each other make more money."

Marcia sent a press release over the wire; it appeared on websites and such notable publications as *Writers' Digest*. Word got around through friends. The initial group that joined comprised people Marcia knew or at least had heard of. Over time, the group has expanded to include people she has never met, which was her initial goal.

"People find me through Google searches, through ASJA, and through conferences," she explains. "A friend of mine was at another conference recently, and she was sitting at a table full of ghostwriters. She said, 'You should look into the Association of Ghostwriters.' Sometimes, that's how it happens.

"I try to explain to people that if you expand your circle of connections, you also expand the potential number of job leads. There are so many opportunities out there, and as we connect with others, our circle gets bigger and bigger and bigger. Why would you want to stay in your own little office surrounded by 250 connections? Why wouldn't you want that to be a million?"

As a member of the Association of Ghostwriters, Bobbi thinks that's a great question.

- **Check your communication skills.** Effective communication has two parts: (1) the basic skills, including listening, speaking, and nonverbal communications; and (2) the ability to structure and manage any discussion, no matter what its subject matter or emotional impact.

The better your listening skills, the better able you will be to connect. Pay attention to how much you're talking. If you're talking nonstop, you are not listening. If you're not listening, you're not attracting connections. You are taking up all the space.

Becoming aware of your own nonverbal communication is not easy. For one thing, you don't see yourself in conversation. You don't know what expression your face is wearing, what your body language is saying without words, and even the effect your posture has on how people perceive you. It's a good idea to ask a friend what nonverbal messages you are sending.

Claudio Diaz, a former trainer with the Walt Disney Institute, once shared with Karen that he had observed that when she was listening intently, she tended to frown. Karen was processing information in her deep-listening mode, completely unaware of her facial expressions. Without Claudio sharing this information, she would have remained unaware of her nonverbal body language.

- **Plan your conversations.** Most people don't think about planning a conversation; they just plunge in and hope for the best. But it pays to give it some thought, especially if you are hoping for a certain outcome. Here is a crash course in how to structure any discussion.

- Think it through. What do you want to achieve? What will not work? What is likely to work?

- Set the stage. Introduce the subject. Present a benefit. Determine willingness to talk.

- Listen first. Ask for the other person's take on the subject. Ask questions. Get emotions out. Summarize content and feelings.

- Then, speak. Create a link from what was just said to what you want to say. Assertively express your views. Use "I" statements.

- Discuss issues. Repeat steps 2, 3, and 4. Go for a win-win.

- Make a plan. What will happen? Who will make it happen? When will it happen? How will you know if the issues are resolved?

- **Be aware of your own energy.** What are you transmitting? Are you a drain on other people's energy or a spark? Do you turn them off or on?

- **Bob Baker** is a modern-day Renaissance man—musician, author, improv humorist, marketing guru, and artist. His energy is amazing and contagious. He keeps things light and makes people laugh. He is genuinely curious and interested in what people do. So, he asks them and usually discovers something he has in common with the person, which sparks an even deeper conversation and connection. Bob is what people call a "natural." Everyone seems to know him, and he is always relaxed and friendly. But that wasn't always the case.

"When I was much younger, I was actually quite awkward at small talk and social interactions," he recalls. "When I did muster the courage to meet people, I made the mistake of wanting to win the approval of everyone I met—especially if I thought they were 'important.'

"I would impatiently wait for them to stop talking so I could launch into rattling off all of my accomplishments and credentials. This was often met with glazed eyes and a sudden need for them to excuse themselves.

"Then an interesting thing happened.

"I started publishing my own music magazine and became a journalist. When I interviewed people, I came prepared with a list of questions and an audio recorder. In these situations, the focus was on my interview subject. So, I got in the habit of asking open-ended questions and doing a lot of listening.

"I was amazed by how much people opened up when they were given an opportunity to talk about themselves—even when they knew they were being recorded and it would end up in print.

"After the interviews were over, my subjects would often say, 'I really enjoyed our conversation.' I felt a real bond with these people. And they had done most of the talking!"

- **Be open to serendipity.** Sometimes, connections find you when you're not even looking for them.

- **Kim Wolterman**, author of *Who's Been Sleeping In My (Bed)room?* and *Keys to Unlocking Your House History*, was walking around the Delmar Loop in St. Louis, Missouri, when she saw a huge, decorated cake sitting on the sidewalk. She snapped a picture and went on her way. Every couple of blocks, she came upon another cake. She kept taking pictures. Kim is a researcher, so she looked into the cake phenomenon and learned that these amazing works of art were strategically placed all over the St. Louis area in celebration of the city's 250th birthday. "My quest to photograph the cakes took me to parts of the city I had never been to and introduced me to people I would never have had the opportunity to meet," says Kim. Eventually, she had 250 photos and a whole new network of other cake lovers who found each other through a Facebook group.

TL250-Cakeway to the West was successful beyond anyone's wildest dreams. "Thousands of people became obsessed with seeing all of the cakes," Kim recalls. "The Facebook group, with more than 2,200 members, took on a life its own. Our first picnic was the start of myriad caking activities. We all like each other, and the group is still going."

From a business perspective, several of the artists have sold their artwork and taught classes in various media. People with different skills have come together to produce calendars, postcards, a book, coasters, and paintings, many of which are available at the Missouriuis History Museum. "It's a thrill for me to see 'Photo by Kim Wolterman' on the back of postcards," says Kim, "but even more exciting to be in an exhibit of cake photographs sponsored by Women in Focus, a group of professional photographers."

- Laura Herring, MA, CRP, GMS, is the founder and chairwoman IMPACT Group, a global, Women's Business Enterprise (WBE)-certified career-development firm, and the author of *No Fear Allowed: A Story of Guts, Perseverance, and Making an Impact.*

When Laura was invited to join a prestigious women's organization, the first annual conference she attended was held in Colombia, South America. On a stationary tourist-restaurant boat, she spent quite a bit of time talking to a woman named Patti. Laura could not have imagined the role this trip and Patti would play in the life of her family.

When Laura returned home, she learned that her nephew, Matt, had just been diagnosed with Hodgkin's lymphoma, stage four. Doctors performed treatment after treatment after treatment, but nothing kept the cancer at bay. Finally, the doctors advised a stem cell replacement. A nationwide search for a donor revealed *only one person* with at least a 50 percent match; that person was Matt's father, John McLane.

Laura recalls, "The only hospital that would even consider a 50 percent match stem cell replacement operation, which was very, very risky, was Johns Hopkins Hospital in Baltimore. Matt had been calling the hospital for two days but had not received a return call. He needed to get this bone marrow transplant done as quickly as possible, and he was beside himself."

It was at that moment that things began to happen because of her connection to a woman she met in South America. Laura called her new friend, Patti, who happened to be the president of Johns Hopkins Heath Systems.

Matt was immediately accepted as a patient at Johns Hopkins but would have to be in quarantine and receive regular treatments in Baltimore for one hundred days. He wondered if Laura knew anyone in Baltimore who could supply his family with housing for three months.

"I had just met about eight women from Baltimore on this trip to Colombia," Laura recalls. A quick email went out to these eight women asking if any of them had a home in Baltimore that they were not using for the winter.

"Emails started flying everywhere. A woman named Suzi Cordish wrote back saying, 'Laura, I know we've never met ... but my son has a guest home on his property that your nephew can use. It is a three-bedroom home, so that all of his family can visit on the weekends.' She refused to accept any payment. What I didn't know," Laura adds, "was that the house had not been lived in for quite some time, so Suzi replaced all of the furniture with new beds and mattresses, living room sofas, etc. She did not want the old furniture to contaminate Matt's sensitive immune system.

"I could not believe it. I had no idea she had done this until many months after they had left her son's home. I had the good fortune to meet Suzi Cordish face to face in Washington, DC, to thank her in person for her generosity."

It is now four years later and, while Matt is not in remission yet, the cancer has not spread. Laura's friendships with the women she met at that conference have grown over the years. "God has a way of guiding you to where you need to be exactly when you need to be there," insists Laura.

You never know where a chance meeting will lead. It could lead to an opportunity to do something you've always wanted to do.

- **Build your brand.** What exactly is a brand? According to **Bob Burg**, co-author of *The Go-Giver*, "It isn't just what you know, and it isn't just who you know.

It's actually who you know who knows you and what you do for a living."

- Two and a half years ago, **Aubrey Betz** was selling radio ads. She was also reading Jeffrey Gitomer's *Little Red Book of Selling* and learning that she should be building her personal brand. She asked herself what she could do to (a) get people to want to meet with her and (b) to tell her about their businesses. What she came up with was the principle of reciprocity.

She would say to prospective customers, "I'll meet with you. I'll buy you a coffee, and I'll write about you and your business. Then, in exchange, you can introduce me to another business owner or another media buyer. So, when I first started, it was to sell advertising, but then I ended up sitting down with a guy who was a former federal prisoner.

"We were drinking tea and eating a panini, and he told me he just gotten out of federal prison. He was very honest about how it happened, and I realized there was a story there. So, by sitting down with people through 'Free Coffee with Aubrey' and hearing their stories, I could see that this was so much bigger than just trying to sell radio ads; this is about connecting with people and hearing their stories. I love meeting people, and I love connecting with them. That's how Free Coffee with Aubrey became my brand."

- **Meet people at a meetup.** Meetup is the world's largest social network of local groups. A meetup group is a local community of people that hosts meetups, which are face-to-face meetings that happen in real life.

- **Will Hanke** is an SEO expert who shares his valuable knowledge at three meetups a month—two at $10 each and one workshop where people bring their laptops and "get stuff done." He's been doing this for a few years, though he has been teaching about SEO for more than a decade. The $10 covers his expenses and assures him of about a 95 percent turnout rate. "There is perceived value when people pay for something," he explains. "But the value isn't just perceived; it is real. We give attendees a lot of very good content to take home and take action on the next day. I want to make sure people get their money's worth twice over." This is his philosophy.

Meetups are the not-so-secret of Will Hanke's business success. "They are a great way for me to meet new people and make business contacts," he says. "I run business ads to try to get people to sign up and attend." Not only does he make valuable contacts for his business, he also helps others connect as well. "People start showing up at about 6:30 pm to have time for networking and conversation before the presentation begins at 7:00. Whether you lead them or attend them, meetups are events where everybody benefits."

- **Meet people at an expo when you are an exhibitor.** You've purchased a table or a booth to showcase your products or services. You may know some of the people who stop by; others may be new to you. This is an opportunity to build brand awareness, conduct market research, and become comfortable speaking extemporaneously.

What to do before an expo

- Start with the end in mind. What are your objectives? Build relationships that can become new clients and customers? Add to your database and build your pipeline to market to new prospects? Build more brand awareness? At the end of the day, were your goals and objectives met?

- Create a master "to-do" list.

- As we suggested in our previous chapter, set aside a block of time AFTER the expo for data entry and follow-up emails.

- Consider creating an email campaign for those who stop by your booth. Create a template email you can personalize for the people you meet and connect with.

- Use social media to tell your community to seek you out at the Expo. Tell them to stop by for a free tip sheet or a giveaway.

- Make sure you get rest! Setting up your booth and

standing on your feet can use a lot of energy!

- Think about what you might do to engage your visitors. What can you do, what can you show, how can you get them to be interested enough to stop and talk to you and to leave their contact info? It could be something interactive, such as a drawing or a survey.

- Rehearse what you want to ask and share with your guests.

- Here is a checklist for what to bring with you when you have a table at an expo:

- A bulleted script to help you stay on track when you talk to visitors

- Signage

- Scissors

- Tape (regular, masking, duct)

- Hammer, nails

- Tacks, push pins

- Stapler

- Fishbowl/box for cards

- Business cards

- Notebook, index cards, tablet, or smart phone for taking notes

- Phone

- Booth schedule for team

- Display items

- Promotional items (pens, etc.)

- Flowers/balloons

- Marketing materials (post cards, brochures, samples)

- Signup sheet for contact info

- Clipboard

- Pens, pencils, markers

- First aid (band aids, aspirin)

- Needle and thread or sewing kit

- Gum/breath mints

What to do at an expo

- Dress the part and wear a SMILE. Keep your positive attitude and most friendly self front and center. This is show time! Try to stay off your phone/computer so you can make eye contact and connections. Consider wearing comfortable shoes and bringing an *extra*-comfortable pair of shoes for late in the day.

- Avoid crossing your arms in front of you while talking to your guests.

- Keep a notebook, tablet, or smart phone on hand to take notes on what you learn from expo guests.

- Be a bit early to set up, so you are relaxed when the expo opens.

- Offer a promotion or a free trial—something that will help create a call to action—an "expo special" or a contest.

- Connect with other exhibitors. Business owners/managers know more people and can help promote you as you promote them.

- Use social media at the event. Use Twitter to invite people to stop by. Tweet about speakers, prizes, etc. Facebook what you are up to. But try to stop by your booth.

- Take care of yourself. Drink water/fluids. Eat. Don't let thirst or hunger rob your energy. Avoid garlicky, strong foods, or keep breath mints on hand.

- Consider having something like chocolate or candy for people to pick up and start a conversation.

What to do after an expo

- How quickly will you follow up? Block out time on your calendar for Monday through Wednesday to call, email, and send something—perhaps a thank you note for stopping by.

- Engage with your visitors on social media. You will stand out from the crowd of faces when you follow through immediately after the event.

- Remember the email you drafted before the expo? Now, it's time to send it out!

- Over the next few weeks, set up appointments to follow up and perhaps meet for coffee.

What to do if you are attending an expo

- Be sure you know where it is. Plug the address into your GPS. If it is in a building, find out where and how to get there.

- Ask for a list and a map of exhibitors; check off the ones you want to visit.

- Have your credit card or checkbook with you in case you want to purchase something.

- Introduce yourself to the person at each table or booth you visit; give her one of your cards; ask for hers; jot a note on the back to remind you of your conversation.

- You probably won't be able to stop at every table or booth, but try to visit the ones you've highlighted on your map.

- Keep the cards all in one place (a plastic bag or an envelope).

- Follow up with an email to everyone with whom you would like to stay in touch, especially if you purchase something.

- Record all new contacts in your database.

How to connect with someone you want to meet

Former TV/film producer, **Jane Ubell-Meyer**, created the world's leading goodie-bag company. She also teaches at Fashion Institute of Technology (FIT) in New York, is CEO and editor in chief of Madison and Mullholland, and on-air talent for Hampton Jitney Magazine TV. Jane knows a lot of people, but the one person she didn't know and wanted to meet was Sir Richard Branson, the founder and CEO of Virgin America.

She had read his autobiography, *How I Lost My Virginity*, written long before he became so well known. When she finished reading it at 4:30 one morning, she woke her husband and declared, "Honey, I love this man. This man is great, and I'm going to get him to call me."

That was the beginning of two years of what might seem to anyone else except Jane to be a series of coincidences. Jane kept running into people who knew someone who knew Branson, and each time she would say, "Just have Richard Branson call me," they would respond, "Not a problem."

These opportunities to meet Richard Branson were always just a bit out of reach. Then, one day, out of the blue, a woman who worked for one of the biggest PR firms in the world called and said, "We just got this assignment to do the launch of Virgin America in four days. We need 250 gift bags. Can you deliver them to us?" This was on a Thursday; the event was on a Monday. Jane said, "yes," on the condition that she would meet Richard Branson. The woman said, "Not a problem."

So Jane delivered the 250 gift bags and met Richard Branson. She told him that *How I Lost My Virginity* was required reading for a class she taught at FIT New York and how it had inspired her to take risks and action in her own life.

To Jane, the story is not about meeting Richard Branson; it is about having a thought in her mind and manifesting what she wanted to happen. "My first goal was getting him to call me," she recalls, "but in that nanosecond when I said it, it was as if it had already happened. I always questioned whether I had glimpsed the future or simply made it happen. I had verbalized a thought, that thought took anchor somewhere, and I followed the clues wherever they took me. When Richard Branson actually called me, that was the culmination of what I call *manifesting to fruition.*

"The core concept of manifesting," Jane explains, "is to have something in your mind and believe it with such intensity that it brings forth the energy around it as if it has already happened. Since I believed that it *had already happened,* making it real was just a matter of taking action. When I let go of worrying about it and freed up the energy I had used for worrying, I could bring it into reality."

Use speed networking to meet a room full of people

According to **Ellen Manus**, a networking expert and event coordinator in Jacksonville, Florida, "With Speed Networking you have a mini business meeting with everyone at the event." Each person has three minutes to explain her service or product, her business needs, and the types of referrals she hopes to get. This is much better than the traditional sixty-second elevator pitch and makes it possible to set up a future meeting if you find a common interest.

The person across from you may not be the perfect client, but he may know someone who is better match. If there is no "connection," you know you only have to endure three minutes. "Speed networking is highly efficient," says Manus. "It allows even the most seasoned business professional to meet people outside of his normal circle of influence."

Here are some things to keep in mind at a speed-networking event:

- Listen to instructions about how people change seats, who talks first, and how long each person gets to speak.

- Smile. For some people this comes naturally. If you're not one of them, you will have to concentrate on doing it.

- If you have an elevator speech, this is the time to use it.

- When it's the other person's turn to speak, pay attention, and listen actively.

- Ask questions, especially those that require more than a yes-or-no answer.

- Take notes or record the conversations on your phone. You are unlikely to remember what is said or who said it.

- Exchange business cards, and write a note on the back if the coating on the card makes that doable.

- At the end of the meeting shake hands, and say thank you. If you said that you would do something, remind both of you that you will do it. Be sure it's written down, and then *do it*.

- Follow up after the event as soon as possible. This will not only make a good impression, it may also create a lasting business connection.

How to attract new connections in the online world

It is often feels as if we live in two worlds—the one on earth we have inhabited all of our lives and the world of cyberspace. Since we discovered the Internet, we've had a lot of company in this new realm—everyone from toddlers to centenarians is playing with a smart phone or a tablet.

- **Websites**

As Bobbi and Karen were finishing this book, they realized that they had completely forgotten another way to make connections—websites. Karen visited a website for an artist named Annie Hurst, and as she was reading it, she saw the word "About." She always goes to the "About" section because she wants to know the people she is dealing with. When she clicked on "About," she read all the normal stuff: "My name is Annie Hurst, I love to create ..."

Annie said a few things about herself: One of them was that she is terrified of goats. She loves animals, but she has this thing about goats. And, yes, as a small child she was traumatized by a goat, but, no, she doesn't want to talk about it. When Karen read that part, she couldn't help but laugh. She suddenly felt "connected" to this woman. Annie has two older brothers who used to torment her relentlessly by handcuffing her to trees, tying her to the clothesline with a jump rope for hours on end, and using her for target practice for their paint ball guns. She got her craftiness and design skills from her dad, who was a landscaper, cattle farmer, and outdoorsman.

"Seriously," she added, "I can't make this stuff up." Karen felt that she was getting to know this woman and really liking that she was so open. The point was that she talked about herself; she talked about her husband and her baby. She said this barely scratched of the surface of what made her who she is. Now when Karen meets her, she will feel as if she already knows her and loves her authentic, fun, and unpretentious style.

- **LinkedIn**

For entrepreneurs, cyberspace is a perfect place to turn casual contacts into profitable connections. Of course, there are many ways to do it, but **Josh Turner**, founder and CEO of LinkedSelling, makes a strong case for focusing on LinkedIn, a business social networking site with 875 million members as of July 2022. We know—Facebook has 2.934 *billion* active users in 2022 and is still growing. An astounding 54% of all Americans have a Facebook account. So, what makes LinkedIn special for those of us who want to build our businesses?

According to a global study conducted by the market research firm IPSOS, LinkedIn was found to be the #1 website visited by the 300,000 people surveyed. These are not just ordinary people; they are the senior-level decision makers in their corporations, the ones who have buying power.

LinkedIn recently noted that 40 percent of its members are on the site daily, really hands on and involved. Those are serious numbers.

What if you are not a corporate, senior-level decision maker but just a small-business owner or a one-man band? How are you going to benefit from LinkedIn (and, for that matter, any other social networking site you join)?

"If you want to position yourself in your market, convey a message, or announce your unique value proposition, LinkedIn is the place to do it," says Josh. There are simple things you can do: Improve your profile. Reach out to other people who are the ones you want to connect with strategically. See the value in connecting with new people. Build connections with people you don't currently know. But, one of the mistakes people often make when they reach out to strangers, Josh notes, is that they don't personalize their invitations to connect. LinkedIn doesn't make that easy. It puts all these people in your face and then doesn't let you customize your message. So, you have to take the extra step on your own.

Here's how: "Visit the person's profile and write a personal note, introduce yourself, mention a mutual friend or a shared interest. Say that you wanted to reach out and connect. That kind of an approach will be far more successful than just clicking the button to get the connection request out. Follow up with a note that says, 'thanks for connecting,' and go a step further with an invitation like this: 'As much as I love social media, I really like to get to know my connections in the real world. Let me know if you're up for a phone call or a cup of coffee sometime.'"

Karen wants to second this. When she speaks to a group, she tells them if they want to connect to her on Facebook or LinkedIn, to please share where they met her. Otherwise, as a general rule, she will not accept Facebook friends or LinkedIn connections. She wants to truly have a "connection" with people in her social media world.

Of course, this is only the tip of the iceberg when it comes to understanding the power and potential of LinkedIn. To go a little deeper, Josh suggests that you get his new book, *Booked: The digital marketing and social media appointment setting system for anyone looking for a steady stream of leads, appointments, and new clients.* where you will learn his system and walk away with a ton of really good content. For more information on LinkedSelling and Josh Turner, see our Resources section.

- **LinkedIn groups**

In July 2008, **Suzi Tozer** started a group on LinkedIn. It was called Event Planners and Coordinators. Suzi's purpose was to find event planners who would help her write her book on great ideas for party planning. People joined the group in order to talk to other event planners, ask questions, and share their knowledge. Suzi's book, *Unforgettable Parties Without Breaking the Bank,* contains thousands of tips from event planners and, according to Suzi, was almost 100 percent written by members of her LinkedIn group. We sadly lost Suzi to breast cancer in January of 2022, but her legacy lives on.

As of October, 2022, the group boasted over 109,000 members. What made it so popular was the free exchange of information and collaboration. "Seasoned event planners were actually giving advice and helping people from other cities with their events and starting or growing their own companies" says Suzi. "For experienced event planners, it was give-back time, and for the inexperienced, it was a time to learn. Because this was an international group, people could ask someone in England a question without fear of competition.

"I think another reason it grew was because I did not have an agenda. I wasn't selling anything. It was purely to help people connect. From the beginning, I encouraged people to interact with each other. Something else that made this grow was that my letters to my members were very personal. I shared my personal struggles and hopes for business, so I became a real person to them."

Suzi's advice to anyone who wants to start a LinkedIn group is to make sure it is something you are interested in because you are going to have to monitor it all the time. She estimates that she works on accepting new members and monitoring discussions at least once a week. "This is going to have to be a subject that you want to talk about for years to come," she advises, "and you will also want to make sure it is something that is broad enough to attract many people.

"This has been my baby—one of the best things I've ever done in my life. I can reach out to any one of these people for advice or to look for a job or to help someone find the resources he needs. You have a different connection when you have met them on LinkedIn."

Bobbi loves writers and is committed to helping them succeed. What better way than to start a group on LinkedIn? WritersWorld, which started with a handful of people, and in 2022 had 9,613 members and growing, which is nowhere near Suzi's group. If you are thinking of starting a group, feel free to borrow any language that is appropriate for you needs. The rules for WritersWorld are fairly loose: *"in order to make this group educational, entertaining, enlightening, and FUN."*

Here are a few of them:

"WritersWorld provides a forum for writers in all genres and at all levels of experience to share ideas, suggestions, questions, experiences, and even rants with others who love the craft as much as you do. We welcome shameless promotion of your writing, business, website, blog, and logo as long as it is in the Promotions section.

"Discussions: You can ask a question, propose a topic, introduce a blog post, or state an opinion. Just be sure you answer these two questions: (1) What is the nature of your post? and (2) How will members benefit from reading it? Be clear, concise, and careful. Don't dash off your posts without rereading them. After all, this is WritersWorld."

True, there are lots of groups for writers on LinkedIn, Facebook, and other sites. The important thing is to visit the ones that seem interesting and relevant to what you do. You may see the same names and posts on several of them because people tend to belong to more than one group. Actually, that is what Bobbi recommends. However, having your name on ten groups but not contributing to nine of them defeats the purpose of social media. It is all about being there, communicating, and forming relationships. You can't do that if you're all over the place. Pick a couple and focus your energy on those. This will position you as a serious professional, not a dilettante.

- **Facebook**

Karen Fox is a certified social-media guru who knows a lot about Facebook. When she started her business more than five years ago, social media was only one of the options she offered her clients. If they wanted to use it, she was all for it. "But it is no longer an option," she says. "It's the place to begin and build from there."

Facebook can seem confusing because it has two ways to connect: a personal page and a business page. "The personal page is all about you and whom you decide to connect with. You choose," Karen explains. "On the business page, you don't get to choose. Those who come to your page are people who have 'liked' it; they are your fans. When they opt in to your page, they are in essence saying, 'Anything you want to share about your page, I am open to hearing.'

"If you are a business, you do need the business page, which also has the advantage of search engine optimization (SEO) and advertising," she adds. "I would absolutely suggest that you advertise, whether you do it once or on an ongoing basis. Advertising on Facebook is reasonably priced, and there are several ways to do it. One way is to target certain people on your list who have already liked your page."

Should you have a Facebook business page or be on LinkedIn? That is the question. According to Karen, there is a different feel to what you post on Facebook and LinkedIn. "Linkedin is typically business to business. To connect with other professionals in your field," says Karen, "I would use LinkedIn. If you are trying to connect with the same people they connect with, I would use Facebook. Start with your friends on Facebook. Ask them to 'like' your business page and to share that information with their friends. A friend list makes it a warm lead. If I trust you, my friends are going to trust you. Ninety-two percent of people will trust a referral from a friend or family member."

Karen highly recommends creating a social media strategy and a calendar. Ask yourself, what am I trying to accomplish here? Do I want to build my brand? Do I want to become a household name? Am I trying to sell my product or service? Or do I just want to lead people back to my website so that they see all the things I have to offer? When you know which way you want to go, fill in your editorial calendar with all the ways you want to send people in that direction.

"This does not have to be an eight-hour-a-day job if you do it correctly. Much of what you need is already on your website," Karen stresses. "All you have to do is break it down and put it on social media according to your strategy and your calendar."

Another Facebook tip comes from **Veronica Grimes**, a partner with L'dara International. Periodically, she goes through her Facebook friends and "likes" their business pages—an effort that is always appreciated.

- **Pinterest**

LinkedIn is personal: Information is exchanged through direct interaction with people. The idea is to connect with people one-on-one on a professional level. What begins as online communication may lead to long-lasting business relationships. Pinterest, on the other hand, is about sharing information through graphics. Contacts or potential contacts interact with images, rather than people. A million people can see what you pin without ever directly making contact.

Bobette Kyle—publisher of MyOnlineWeddingHelp.com , a website for wedding planning on a limited budget, and AspirationalBride.com, a site for brides who aspire to create their perfect wedding—swears by Pinterest. It works for her big time, with 3.2 million monthly viewers, over 70.4K followers, and 180,000 people a month who act on her pins, and 459,000 daily impressions of pins from her website.

"The wedding industry does well on Pinterest," says Bobette. "Women who are planning weddings are very visual, and Pinterest is the most visual of social media platforms." In addition to her own boards, she has established one on which other professionals in the industry—competitors, service providers, and vendors—also pin ideas and products.

People interact with Pinterest in various ways: They buy things, they learn about things, and they learn how to do things. The value of Pinterest to Bobette is that "all of these people come in contact with my business, and that drives traffic to my website, which increases my revenue."

- **YouTube**

It's one thing to put a funny or crudely made video up on YouTube to entertain your friends, but it is quite another to use this powerful medium as a vehicle to achieve your business objectives. Best-selling author, keynote speaker, and entrepreneur **Mason Duchatschek** is an expert on using YouTube with that in mind.

Here's what you should know

- Exactly what you want to accomplish

- How to create content that will be found by your ideal prospects, customers, and influencers who are looking for your particular expertise

- The questions your ideal prospects ask most often (answer them on video) Also known as your FAQ section

- The questions your ideal prospects SHOULD be asking (answer them on video)

Mason follows that advice with what you should *do*. Make sure that every piece of content you create is a positive representation of you and your brand, because there is no "erase" button on the Internet. Choose your words carefully. The words you use in your titles, description, and content matter, because they are picked up by search engines.

Struggling with whether to have a professional video made or going the do-it-yourself route? "These aren't mutually exclusive choices," says Mason. "Each type of video has its place. Just make sure the video quality is congruent with your image and the theme of the content.

"If you do record your own video," he advises, "keep it simple. iMovie is REALLY easy if you have a Mac. Use a teleprompter. (There are apps for both the iPhone and iPad that work great. I'm a fan of Teleprompt+). Practice. Don't worry about being perfect; just focus on being genuine and authentic."

Camera-shy? There's a simple solution: Buy a USB microphone, such as "Nessie" by Blue, and add a voiceover to any presentation on your computer screen. You can record it easily using software like Screenflow (Mac) or Camtasia (PC).

Final word of advice from Mason: If you don't own a Mac, he would encourage you to buy one.

How to stay connected

Here are some things to keep in mind. First, don't be overwhelmed by these suggestions. You can't do everything. You can't constantly stay in touch with everyone you meet unless this is your passion in life (as it is Karen's) or your business strategy. Do what's appropriate when the mood strikes you or an opportunity pops up.

- Find places you like to go to with people you like to hang out with. You never know who else you might meet there.

- If   you   keep   up   with   Facebook   announcements—birthdays, events, invites, or tragedies—send a real card, an e-card, an email, or a note on the person's wall conveying heart-felt wishes, congratulations, or condolences.

- If you see an article of interest to one of your connections, cut it out and put it in the mail, or cut and paste and put the link in an email. If you see someone mentioned in the news, clip it, and send it with a brief congratulatory note.

- Introduce your connections to each other or to people you know.

- Don't lose your connections. Enter business card info and notes into your database immediately. (See Resources.)

- Don't think of any networking event you attend as a one-time occurrence; think of it as the beginning of the contacts-connections-collaboration process. You never know when a new connection can help you or someone you know.

- Follow up on promises or information you offered to send. It shows you care and builds credibility immediately.

- Use the business cards and notes you have collected to connect on LinkedIn, Facebook, and other social networking sites.

- Send someone a book you particularly like. Put it in the mail with a note or buy a gift card on Kindle or some other e-reader.

How to make connections deeper

When Karen meets people and really likes them, she wants to stay connected, to reach out and see about possibly getting together. She will try to find them on Facebook so that they can start being Facebook friends. The whole Facebook phenomenon has been incredible for getting to go deeper because she sees things that are going on for a lot of people who use Facebook. So, if something cool happens in their business and they talk about it, Karen can comment on that. If there is something personal going on, she offers a prayer or congratulations or condolences.

The other way to make deeper connections is when you are one-on-one with someone, and you are really listening to what is going on with that person. Karen's first impulse is to want to know how she can help. She may not say that when she is talking to people, but that is what she is listening for. If somebody tells a story about what is happening in his life or business, she tries to help him make connections. Knowing more about people—their dreams, their goals, their challenges—deepens relationships. We have talked about this in other parts of the book: When you reach out with a card or clip an article or send a link to somebody, it shows him that you are thinking of him and that you really care.

What is a connector?

- According to Malcolm Gladwell, author of *The Tipping Point*, connectors are people who link us up with the world ... "People with a special gift for bringing the world together ... They are a handful of people with a truly extraordinary talent for making friends and acquaintances." Gladwell attributes the social success of connectors to "their ability to span many different worlds ... A function of something intrinsic to their personality, some combination of curiosity, self-confidence, sociability, and energy."

- Connectors collect people. They have a genuine interest in and love for other people. Connectors go beyond those they know well and have many ties outside of their inner circle.

- Connectors are matchmakers. They put people together for a variety of reasons: to form a business relationship or to find help with specific jobs, such as wedding planning, baby sitting, or house cleaning. They see the matches in their mind's eye. They know when two people *have* to meet. There is something strategic about why these people have to meet. Karen likens it to having a Rolodex in her brain that knows when she has to introduce people to each other.

- Karen does email introductions with "Karen Hoffman Introduction" in subject line. She doesn't like to do phone introductions. She prefers to send an email intro to both parties, in which she does a brief synopsis of each person's relevant info and the reasons why they should connect. These are usually strategic introductions, but Karen also has learned to trust her intuition and will make connections that "feel" right, with great results.

- According to Dale Carnegie, "You can close more business in two months by becoming interested in other people than you can in two years by trying to get people interested in you."

- A connector is an expert at facilitating introductions. Anybody can learn to do this via email, phone, LinkedIn, Facebook, at a party, or at a formal networking event. Karen does "strategic connections" that have an underlying purpose that could benefit both parties.)

Because of an article in the *St. Louis Business Journal*, Karen was able to successfully connect two non-profit organizations with surprising results.

Here's how it happened: Karen was at a conference on innovation when she realized that one of the speakers was Michael Holmes, someone she had read about in the paper. Michael had started a non-profit called RxOutreach to help people with limited income get the prescription drugs they need at affordable prices. Karen had torn the page out of the *St. Louis Business Journal* because she hoped to meet Michael someday. He was as delightful in person as the article portrayed him to be, and she knew that she wanted to connect him with one of her friends who also had a non-profit. Karen took Michael out to Connections to Success to meet its founders, Kathy and Brad Lambert.

Then, Kathy introduced Michael to Scott Anders, Deputy Chief, U.S. Probation of the U.S. District Court, Eastern District of Missouri. When people are released from prison, they are given two weeks' worth of their prescription drugs, but it sometimes takes four to six weeks to get in to see a doctor for a new prescription. What often happens is that former prisoners run out of their medication before they can get more. Kathy introduced Michael to Scott, and Michael and Scott teamed up to help people coming out of prison. That was not even on the radar but has resulted in creating a program for those released from prison to have their medications for an extended period of time.

All Karen had wanted to do was connect Kathy and Michael to help Kathy's clients who are welfare moms and women who have been in prison. This one little connection turned out to help many more people than anyone could have predicted.

How do you find connectors?

- Who do you know who seems to know everyone, has a deep interest in people, and has a burning desire to connect people? There aren't many, but those who fit this description were born that way. You see them making introductions at live events, telling someone, "*You have to meet* so and so because..." and using social media to put their friends together. Connectors like to promote other people but not themselves. They know that it's not about them.

- Places to look for them, groups who may have them: Consider professional groups, restaurant owners, headhunters, lobbyists, fundraisers, politicians, journalists, and people who keep showing up all over social media. These are not necessarily connectors, but they are good places to start. These people have a lot of connections but don't always share whom and what they know.

- Don't assume that connectors are all extroverts; introverts can be great connectors. It's a wiring issue. They think of who can help someone else and try to introduce them to each other. They listen. They care about what you're saying. They sometimes take notes because it helps them think of whom they want to introduce you to.

How do you learn to become a connector?

First, it's very helpful if you have some basic personality traits. Ask yourself these questions and be honest with your answers.

- Do you genuinely like people? Do you look for the good in them?

- Do you collect people? Do you have an abundance of friends?

- Do you introduce your friends to your other friends?

- Are you a glass-is-half-full person, able to find a silver lining in most situations?

- Do you radiate positive energy? Do you smile often?

- Are you aware of other people's interests, passions, or concerns? Do you care about them?

- If you answered yes to some of those questions, you have what it takes to be a connector.

Second, you must be willing to invest yourself in relationships. That requires:

- Having a mindset that relationships really matter.

- Listening to people at a deeper level in order to *hear* them.

- Taking the time to follow up and stay connected. Some things take only moments to do (a quick email); other things take much longer (meeting one on one).

- Doing whatever you do with a giver's heart. Don't expect anything in return.

- Specific examples: Use social media. If you notice someone hosting an event, share it. If you see someone getting an award, congratulate her. Make it personal; be specific about what you're congratulating her for.

- Read newspapers, magazines, social networking headlines, online sites. You may find something that can help someone. Notice as you read if there is someone you might want to get to know.

Leveraging connections to build your business

Debbie Champion is a partner in Rynearson Suess Schnurbusch & Champion, LLC (RSSC), a St. Louis law firm. She is also a realist. "If I am really honest with myself," she says, "I have to admit that we are NOT the only ones who can serve the needs of our clients. When I was new in the business, I could not imagine why people would want to use anyone else to handle their business! However, as time has gone on, I realize that our services are widely available. There are lots of great attorneys who can do the job and many as well as I can.

"So the thing that differentiates you from your competition is YOU and your connection to your clients. Whether that is a personal connection, a family connection, or just an introduction by some mutual acquaintance. If you do not have a connection of some sort to your client, then you don't have the client. And if you don't maintain that connection to your client, you won't obtain new business from that client."

Debbie is a prolific note writer. As incredibly busy she is with her law practice, she always seems to have a few note cards with her to send out at the appropriate moment. If she is sitting somewhere with nothing to do, she will start writing. Karen is sure those notes help Debbie stay connected to her clients and friends.

Besides connections, Debbie credits her team for RSSC's success. "We are highly rated attorneys who have the best litigators in the area and are extremely competitive on price. But no matter how good we are, or how reasonably priced we are, it is not one attorney who makes us successful; it is our TEAM that sets us apart. You are only as strong as your weakest link, and I surround myself with people who have different ideas and different strengths than mine and who are not afraid to pursue a problem in a manner I might not consider. Given the same case, the same problems, I never doubt that my team will perform the best over the long haul."

Where do you start?

Just ask someone, "What is it that could help you in your life? In your job? In your business? In your family? To reach a particular goal?" It doesn't have to be fulfilling her dream. It could be finding a solution to a particular problem. Ask directly, "How can I help you?" People have needs they think they have to handle by themselves. Be open to how something can surface that isn't tied to money.

Often, people think if I just had money, it would make everything better. There is this myth that money is the answer to everything. But often people don't have money to give. They might have time or a barter opportunity or a way to work together. We must be open to how something can show up that can lead to collaboration. Collaboration is about how we can come together with our gifts and our talents and our connections to make something happen. Money buys you stuff; collaboration builds community. Something happens when people share their gifts. Think back to the time when families came together for barn raisings. In the space of a day, they could put up a barn for a neighbor in need. They didn't have money. They had strength, generosity, spirit, and lots of food. A barn raising was a party. It was a community collaboration.

Share with others what you are looking for

We are not naturally inclined to share our innermost yearnings. We're not wired to go around telling people what we need or want or dream of doing. We're actually wired more to keep that stuff to ourselves unless we are with a close friend. Here are some of the reasons you might hesitate to share your dreams:

- You're worried about how you look to others.

- You don't want to appear dumb, not really knowing enough about your subject to discuss it intelligently.

- You may feel vulnerable sharing a big dream; there are people out there who may want to keep your dream small or who may smash it. They are the naysayers, more than willing to tell you all the reasons you can't achieve it.

- You are concerned about taking up time and space

when someone else could be sharing her dream.

- It may be that you simply don't know what you want.

- You may be afraid to dream, feeling that don't deserve what you secretly yearn for.

- You haven't given energy to figuring out what you want.

- You don't know where you could possibly make a difference in the world.

- You think you will be ridiculed for reaching so high.

- You are too modest to toot your own horn.

Why should you do it anyway?

Your life can change in a nanosecond just by sharing what you need with the right, positive-thinking person and having him become a resource. Everyone has ideas and information. Everybody has a past full of experiences and connections and stuff they know. You don't know what they've done, where they've been. When you open up, you find out.

It might be a business that has a particular requirement, but often, it is just that someone who has a need: a friend who is looking for somebody to clean her house, and you know just the right person; a client who is planning a wedding, and you just met a great wedding planner; a neighbor who is looking for a babysitter or someone to work on her car. It could be anything. Everybody needs ideas, information, and introductions to help them along. Connectors love to share ideas, information, and introductions; so, it's a perfect marriage. How do you do it?

- Be on the lookout for people who are "heart smart," kind, and open to positive possibilities. They are not going to tell you all the reasons why it *can't* work; they are going to point out all the reasons why it *can* work.

- Stay away from the naysayers. Learn how to coach people and model the behavior and language you *do* want, not what you *don't* want. Be for them what you want them to be for you.

- Become a champion. A champion is an advocate, a supporter. When you are a champion, you believe in someone, you want to help him succeed, to make a difference in his life. You start listening for opportunities to make connections for him, to share things with him that are going to help him achieve his goals, whether they are business or personal.

- Sometimes, others see your dream more clearly than you do. One of Karen's favorite quotes is: *"When I see in you what you do not see in yourself, I am the bridge."* Karen is a bridge. Sometimes, you don't see that dream for yourself, and you need someone else to see it for you. That's what coaches do. That is the purpose of Gateway to Dreams: It holds space for people's dreams.

- **Glenda Woolley** is a dream champion. She believes that we are all here for a purpose. "Each of us has a longing or a desire or something we dreamed of doing one day," Glenda says. "At Gateway to Dreams we invite people to revisit their dreams. Sometimes, they are buried so deep, people didn't ever believe they were possible." What Glenda loves about Gateway to Dreams is that it gives people the hope that they can resurrect their idea or dream from long ago. It doesn't have to be starting a business. Sometimes,it is going back to school. Other times, it is just wanting to self-develop."

- Karen and a group of entrepreneurs and business professionals in St. Louis who wanted to help people connect with the resources they need to realize their dreams created Gateway to Dreams (G2D), which is all about ideas, information, and introductions. The group hosts events to help people make connections, as well as having several regular programs.

- Joy of Goals is a workshop that helps people get in touch with their dreams and to establish an atmosphere of collaboration.

- Connecting and Promoting Women is a group whose purpose is to help women make more meaningful and strategic connections, meeting monthly and on Zoom.

- Every program Gateway to Dreams creates is intended to help make connections and help create more opportunities for collaboration.

- Write Your Book Right Now is a monthly program via Zoom with interviews of authors and action-taking steps to meet writing goals.

Conclusion

Connections are the lifeblood of any business of any size in any industry. Can you imagine a business where who you know doesn't matter? And the more people who know you, the more you and your brand are visible to the world. The more people you know, the more people you can help. People begin to think of you as the go-to person in your field, and you know right where to turn when you need something. Your world expands to encompass new perspectives, new opportunities, new business prospects, new friendships, new collaborations.

MEMORABLE QUOTES

"A GREAT ATTITUDE DOES MUCH MORE than turn on the lights in our worlds; it seems to magically connect us to all sorts of serendipitous opportunities that were somehow absent before the change." —*Earl Nightingale*

"People are opportunities. The gift is in the interaction and the connection with another person, whether it lasts forever or not." —*Colleen Seifert*

"Only when one is connected to one's own core is one connected to others." —*Anne Morrow Lindbergh*

"Why is it in a country as wealthy as we are, that we lack a sense that our lives are part of some greater effort, that we are connected to one another?" —*Hillary Rodham Clinton*

"Since you cannot do good to all, you are to pay special attention to those who, by accidents of time, or place, or circumstances, are brought into closer connection to you." —*St. Augustine*

"Creativity is the power to connect the seemingly unconnected." —*William Plomer*

"We cannot live only for ourselves. A thousand fibers connect us with our fellow men." —*Herman Melville*

"The beginning of a friendship, the fact that two people out of the thousands around them can meet and connect and become friends, seems like a kind of magic to me. But maintaining a friendship requires work. I don't mean that as a bad thing. Good art requires work as well." —*Charles de Lint*

"Your intuition will tell you where you need to go; it will connect you with people you should meet; it will guide you toward work that is meaningful for you—work that brings you joy, work that feels right for you." —*Shakti Gawain*

"… More people in more places can now compete, connect, and collaborate with equal power and equal tools than ever before." —*Thomas Friedman*

"It is in giving that I connect with others, with the world, and with the divine." —*Isabel Allende*

"Connection is why we're here. We are hardwired to connect with others; it's what gives purpose and meaning to our lives, and without it there is suffering." — *Brené Brown*

QUICK REMINDERS

Differences Between

Contacts and Connections

Contact	Connection
• The first step, an introduction, an exchange of basic information (name, profession, company name) • May not even be face-to-face • Casual, surface knowledge	• More personal, in-depth • Has the potential for a relationship • The feeling of a connecting link or "hot pink thread"
• Can be pleasant and fun • Kind of a "Hi, how are you? If I see him again, that's fine; if I don't, that's fine, too."	• Someone I could grow to care about • Someone I would like to see again • The beginning of a friendship

How To Become A Connector

To be a connector, you:	To invest in relationships, you:	Try these things:
• Genuinely like people. • Look for the good in everyone. • Collect people. • Introduce your friends to your other friends. • Are a glass-is-half-full person. • Find a silver lining in most situations. • Radiate positive energy. • Smile often. • Care about others. • Are aware of their interests, passions, concerns.	• Believe that relationships matter. • Listen to people at a deeper level. • Take the time to meet someone's needs. (Some things take only moments; others take much longer.) • Do what you do with a giver's heart; don't expect anything in return.	• On social media, if you read that someone is getting an award, congratulate him or her. • Make it personal; be specific about what the congratulations are for. • Read newspapers, magazines, social-networking headlines, online sites. • Look for something that can help someone. • Follow through on your promises and commitments.

Choosing the Right Social Media

Social Media Site	Why Use It
• **LinkedIn**: World's largest professional network; an online service that helps professionals find and connect with one another through shared social contacts	• To attract attention of senior-level decision makers who have buying power • To build your network • To make connections through special-interest and industry groups • To share your experience, academic and professional credentials, and accomplishments
• **Facebook Biz Page**: Allows you to promote your business, create profit, connect and engage with customers, and amplify your voice	• To increase exposure to potential customers • To build brand loyalty • To generate more leads • To reduce marketing expenses • To boost your SEO
• **Pinterest**: About sharing information through graphics. Contacts or potential contacts interact with images, rather than people	• To increase your credibility • To enhance your social presence • To grow the size of your audience • To drive traffic to your site • To reach new customers
• **YouTube**: A website, owned by Google, on which users can post, view, or share videos	• To take advantage of the 2nd largest search engine in the world • To be found on Google and reach a worldwide audience • To encourage viewers to promote you and buy from you • To make your videos available to others

COLLABORATION

"Isolation is the fastest path to insanity; collaboration is the fastest path to success." —Lethia Owens

⸺◆⸺

THIS CHAPTER IS ABOUT collaboration: what it is, how it grows from connections into something deeper, how to find heart-smart collaboration partners, how to create win-win situations, and why it's important to share your goals and dreams with others.

Collaboration defined

In its simplest form, collaboration occurs when two or more people work together to achieve a shared mission or goal. But to collaborate also means:

Being an active member of the team

Helping each other

Harnessing the power of collective intelligence

Creating synergy

Brainstorming to solve a problem

Building relationships

Seeing the big picture

Being inspired

Leaving one's ego at the door

The difference between a connection and collaboration

Connection is a relationship in which you are linked in some way to another person. You have some things in common. You feel energized by conversations, being in each other's company. You resonate with her energy, her attitude. You like each other, but you're not working on anything together—a project or a goal. *Collaboration* is coming together to help each other achieve a mutual objective, create something new, bring out each person's best thinking and effort, and take a project from concept to completion. Connections are a way to BE with another person. Collaboration is what you and that person DO to achieve something greater than either of you could achieve alone.

How to turn a connection into collaboration

Over time, you become comfortable with each other. You explore each other's dreams and projects to see if you have things in common. You look for an opportunity to help each other. Strategic collaboration is about knowing that there is something you are going to work on together. It is purposeful: You look for that "something." You explore its possibilities. You create a plan. On the other hand, not all combined efforts are so well thought out. There is also serendipitous collaboration, which is more accidental. It just happens, takes shape, and becomes something you weren't expecting. But its very spontaneity can energize you and bring some real excitement to everything you do together.

What collaboration produces that you couldn't produce on your own

Creativity is a mysterious process. An artist or inventor or scientist takes existing elements—ideas, materials, words—throws them into a pot, stirs them around for a while, and ultimately produces a completely original product. When two or more people pool their talents and knowledge, the contents of the pot and the possibilities they may yield multiply exponentially. We can never completely grasp how that product is unlike anything that went into that pot or, in fact, unlike anything else in the world. It doesn't matter what goes in; what comes out is always unique. This is the power of collaboration.

Keith Sawyer, PhD, Morgan Distinguished Professor in Educational Innovations at the University of North Carolina at Chapel Hill, puts a new spin on the importance of collaboration. "Creativity is *always* collaborative," he insists, "even when you're alone." In his 2007 book, *Group Genius: The Creative Power of Collaboration*, Dr. Sawyer debunked many time-honored myths about creativity.

"We have this belief that our moments of insight happen when we're alone, while we're meditating or exercising or gardening," he wrote. "What we're learning form empirical studies is that this is *not* the way creativity happens. There is never a flash of insight. What actually happens is that there are many small moments of insight that are interspersed with constant periods of collaboration and interaction. Our moments of insight are manifestations of those collaborations."

One of the myths we seem to treasure is that of the solitary genius who suddenly has an epiphany and produces or invents something completely original. Forget it, says Sawyer.

"Nothing innovative ever comes from the mind of one solitary genius. We are told such stories because they are easier to remember as a kind of shorthand. Scratch beneath the surface, and you'll find the real historical facts. Samuel Morse did *not* invent the telegraph. Thomas Edison did *not* invent the light bulb. There is no evidence that Mozart wrote whole symphonies without a single correction. TS Eliot's 'Wasteland' was radically edited before it was ever published."

Sawyer's group collaboration theory was somewhat radical in 2007 but has become almost standard thinking as new books, such as *How to Fly a Horse, The Innovators,* and *Where Do Good Ideas Come From,* have come out on the subject.

In a collaborative team, members play off one another. Whatever comes out is a group effort. What is absent is the ego. Members of a collaborative group are focused on the best possible outcome for the project or goal or group; they are *not* focused on what's in it for each of them as individuals.

Collaborative intelligence

Most of us have heard of IQ (intelligence quotient) and SQ (social intelligence quotient), but a new term that is gaining prominence in the business lexicon is C-IQ (collaborative intelligence quotient). C-IQ measures how well we are able to think with others, as opposed to alone. As business changes its emphasis, new trends emerge, and one that is gaining traction is "mind sharing." Today, market leaders wield *influence* rather than *power*, and success increasingly results from collaboration and the ability to inspire.

Dawna Markova's book, *Collaborative Intelligence,* is the culmination of more than fifty years of original research in cognitive neuroscience. She and her "thinking partner," Angie McArthur, have exposed some of the world's top CEOs and creative professionals to this concept. They are experts at getting brilliant yet difficult people to think together and have helped many leaders resolve crises and inspire their teams.

In working with Fortune 500 companies, Markova and McArthur have found that managers who appreciate intellectual diversity and employees and teams who understand it will work together in a spirit of harmony to come up with new ideas and create innovative solutions to problems.

Lethia Owens is ranked eighth among the top thirty branding gurus in the world according to Global Gurus. She helps people uncover their unique talents and genius—what they have to contribute to the world. "So often, people have hit obstacles on the road and been knocked down. Sometimes, they are too discouraged to get back up," says Owens.

This was the case with a young woman named Gloria who had attended the Christian Songwriters Conference in St. Charles, Missouri, in 2007. Michael, a classically trained pianist, was also at the conference. People had traveled from all over the world to come to this conference, Michael told Lethia. Everyone was at lunch when he caught sight of Gloria, who was sitting quietly alone. Michael grabbed his lunch and went over to her table to talk to her. He asked her how she was doing. She said, I'm okay, but she clearly was far from okay. After some prodding, Gloria finally shared her story with Michael. "For years," she confessed, "I have had this song in my heart, and every time I work with someone to try and get that song out, it just never comes out the way that I hear it in my head."

So, Michael asked her to come over to the piano with him. "I would love to just play around and see if I can come up with something that would match your song." Gloria refused. "No Michael, you don't understand," she insisted. "I've tried far too many times, and I just couldn't do it again." Michael must have been persuasive because eventually, Gloria gave in. As she and Michael sat on the piano bench, she closed her eyes and began to sing. As she sang, Michael tapped on the keys trying to find the perfect notes. After a while, Gloria forgot Michael was there. She was singing, and Michael was playing;

the result was Gloria's song. At the end, she was in tears, and he was all smiles.

This unexpected collaboration was just what it took to bring Gloria's song to life. "I love that story," says Lethia. "I tell it all the time. The point I'm always trying to make is when you have something inside of you that you want to bring forth, that you want to share with the world, often it's going to take more than just you to make it happen." When Gloria's gift of singing her own song merged with Michael's gift of musical composition, the result was something magical that neither of them could have created without the other. When gifts collide amazing things happen.

Maxine Clark, best known for her Build-A-Bear franchise, spent twenty-five years in the retail business, eventually becoming president of Payless Shoe Source, a division of the May Department Stores Company. Payless Shoesource was one of the largest sellers of shoes in America, and while she was there, Maxine made many connections with the vendors who made shoes for her company. The relationships were always give-and- take, and very successful.

When Maxine left Payless Shoesource, she didn't know exactly what she would do next, but she did know she wanted to stay in touch with people who had helped her become successful. She had also helped them, by the way.

In 1997, she launched the first Build-A-Bear store at the Saint Louis Galleria in St. Louis, Missouri. Today, there are more than four hundred stores worldwide and 125 million furry friends around the globe.

"About a year after our first store opened," recalls Maxine, "one of those vendors who had been incredibly helpful to us at Payless Shoesource and became a friend, looked at our business plans. He thought it was great that we were talking about having shoes. He said, 'When you are ready for shoes, call me. I will make it happen, regardless of how small the quantity is.' This company was right here in St. Louis where we are, and it makes millions of pairs of shoes for Wal-Mart, Payless, Target, and other stores all over. And then, it made shoes for us.

"Years later, my friend called me and said, 'I just want you to know that in January, we shipped more shoes to you than we shipped to Wal-Mart.' This was pretty amazing because bears wear shoes only when it rains and snows, right?

"There is another great shoe story: We had opened up store number thirty-three in California, and another one of my friends in the shoe business had just come out with Skechers. He went to that mall where our new store was located, and he saw all these kids were in there wearing Skechers shoes and buying our bears. He thought it would be a good idea for Build-A-Bear to consider carrying Skechers shoes for the bears.

"I said great! How much you going to charge me for those shoes? His reply? 'Nothing. Let's do it for a year and see how it goes. If it is successful, we will talk about what you should pay.' By the next day he had sent me all the best styles. A year later, we negotiated a great contract. This was a wonderful relationship born out of a trust.

"The Skechers promotion was incredibly successful. The cutest thing was that kids wanted to have shoes just like the bears."

Collaborations that made or changed history

- **Amnon Amir, Sefi Vigiser, Arik Vardi, Yair Goldfinger, and Yossi Vardi**: The fathers of instant messaging (IM) started out in an industrial garage in Tel Aviv. With $75,000 in seed money, Mirabilis' ICQ went online in December 1996. Within six weeks, it had 30,000 users; six months later, one million; and by 1998, twelve million. AOL bought the company for $400 million in cash—a watershed moment for the Internet and Israel's then-fledgling high-tech industry.

- **Coco Chanel and Pierre Wertheimer**: In 1924, three years after creating her iconic fragrance, Chanel No. 5, Coco Chanel partnered with Pierre Wertheimer, a successful French businessman, to help her establish Parfums Chanel. The deal made Chanel a wealthy woman, but today, the Wertheimer family owns 100 percent of the company, including worldwide rights to the Chanel name. Chanel No. 5 remains one of the best-selling perfumes in history.

- **Ben Cohen and Jerry Greenfield**: While their product may not have changed the world, Ben and Jerry's ice cream, with its chunky texture and rich taste, has led a veritable ice cream revolution. Not only were they among the first to mass-produce so-called premium ice cream but they were also one of the first food companies to adopt sustainable practices. Making the world a better place with chunks of fudge brownie and chocolate chip cookie dough is definitely one great example of a successful collaboration.

- **Thomas Edison, J.P. Morgan, and the Vanderbilts**: Invented by Thomas Edison and funded by a group of wealthy investors, including J.P. Morgan and the Vanderbilt family, the incandescent electric light bulb helped lay the groundwork for the Edison Electric Light Co. In 1882, the first commercial central power system was installed in Manhattan. By 1887, 121 Edison central power stations spanned the country.

- **Bill Gates and Paul Allen**: The founders of Microsoft met and became friends at Lakeside School in Seattle. Realizing the future of micro-processing and that writing and selling software was the new frontier, they created Microsoft BASIC, the first high-level programming language. This led to one of the most successful and largest U.S. corporations in history, as well as making Gates and Allen two of the richest people in the world.

- **Bill Hewlett and David Packard**: Starting with $538

and a used drill press in a rented Palo Alto garage, Hewlett and Packard developed the HP200A, an audio oscillator designed to test sound equipment. Hewlett-Packard is known for innovative tech products, as well as its open corporate culture and management style. By 1942, HP had $522,803 in yearly revenue. Today the company that introduced laser jet printers, touch screens, and personal computers is a global behemoth with $104.3 billion in annual sales.

- **Steve Jobs and Steve Wozniak:** The co-founders of Apple created computers that changed history. Reportedly launched in a garage in 1976, Apple Inc., now a multinational corporation known for recognizable products and simple design, creates consumer electronics, computer software, and media content.

- **John Lennon and Paul McCartney:** When Lennon and McCartney started writing and recording songs together as part of the Beatles, they had no idea how far their partnership would take them. The Beatles was one of the most influential bands in history, and Lennon and McCartney's dynamic creative partnership created a sound that changed popular music forever.

- **Richard and Maurice McDonald:** In the late 1920s, the New Hampshire-born brothers moved to California and opened a barbecue restaurant where they gained the experience they would later use to pioneer the fast-food industry. They focused on a simple menu, quality, and fast service. In 1954, Ray Kroc purchased the entire business and the rights to the McDonald's name for $2.7 million. Today, there are 31,000 Golden Arches around the globe that take in $22.7 billion a year.

- **Paul Otlet and J.C.R. Licklider:** (collaboration across the decades). Belgian information expert Paul Otlet envisioned a worldwide, networked knowledge base. Originally, his "Universal Bibliographic Repertory" was on physical cards and people queried and received answers by mail. As new technologies, such as microfilm, came into being, he integrated them into the knowledge base. Most important, he theorized, as early as the 1930s, about conveying information through radio, television, and telephone signals. The Internet, as we know it, really got started in the early 1960s. J.C.R. Licklidera—a computer scientist with the technology company, Bolt, Beranek, and Newman (BBN) and one of the developers of ARPANET, a direct precursor of the Internet—described an "Intergalactic Computer Network" that would link computers together across the globe.

- **Larry Page and Sergey Brin:** After dropping out of Stanford, Page and Brin set up shop in a friend's garage, experimented with search algorithms, and raised about $1 million in capital. Initially, they received 10,000 queries a day; today, that number is estimated at 235 million. The world's No. 1 Internet search engine, Google, earned $16.5 billion in sales. Its founders never dreamed that their company would become an integral part of the lives of millions.

- **Richard Rogers and Oscar Hammerstein**: After long and highly distinguished careers with other collaborators, Richard Rodgers (composer) and Oscar Hammerstein II (librettist/lyricist) joined forces to create the most consistently fruitful and successful partnership in the American musical theatre.

- **Martin Siegfried and Roy Horn**: Sons of fathers who were abusive alcoholics and soldiers in Hitler's army, Siegfried and Roy were determined to leave their difficult pasts behind them. They met on an ocean liner where they both had jobs and discovered their shared passion for magic and performing before live audiences. They became the most sold-out, profit-producing show in Las Vegas history, with annual revenues of $36 million.

- **Sam, Jack, Albert, and Harry Warner**: Sons of Polish-born Jewish immigrants, these brothers co-founded what would become Warner Bros. Studios. Over the years, they worked in film production and distribution, ran a traveling movie business, established their own movie house, and produced their own films. Sam Warner is credited with ending the silent film era in 1927 with the first feature-length talkie, *The Jazz Singer*. The blockbuster film, which grossed some $3 million, established Warner Bros. as a major player and revolutionized the film industry.

- **James Watson and Francis Crick**: Building on the work of chemist Dr. Rosalind Franklin, Drs. Watson and Crick described the double helix that forms the framework for the basic building blocks of all life. In so doing, they laid the foundation for understanding the human genome.

- **The Wright brothers**: In 1903, Wilbur and Orville Wright developed the three-axis controls that made flying a fixed-wing aircraft possible. Their invention opened the world to the kind of travel most people had only dreamed about and changed the face of travel.

How collaborations develop

Sometimes, they take some time, as people become better acquainted and aware of how they might work together. Bobbi and Peggy Nehmen met at St. Louis Publishers Association (SLPA) several years ago. They didn't know each other well until they collaborated on a book for one of Bobbi's clients. That book led to another and another and another, and eventually to Peggy becoming Bobbi's "go-to" book designer. Peggy designed the last eight of Bobbi's books and created a brand for her online course and promotional materials. On the other hand, Peggy needed an editor for some of her clients and her own writing. As this collaboration deepened, they referred each other to their clients and have worked on more than twenty-two book projects together. They share a seamless and very successful collaboration.

What collaboration looks like when it works

Karen and Bobbi's collaboration on this book was completely spontaneous. Their contact happened many years ago but never developed beyond that—until 2014—when it took off like a jackrabbit. The connection was immediate, and the collaboration on a book began shortly after their first meeting. Sometimes, it just happens that way. What made this collaborative effort work so well was that Karen and Bobbi brought different strengths to the table.

Karen is the queen of connections. She knows a million people (or so it seems) and can recite all of their resumes from memory. She can talk about the subject of connecting people for hours with no notes but has trouble sitting still long enough to put her thoughts on paper. She is much more a natural speaker than a writer. What Karen needed was to work with someone who could organize a lot of information, interview her to capture her thoughts and expertise, and help convey what she wants to say exactly as she would say it if she could. That's the approach she took with her first book, *The*

Art of Barter, which she wrote with business reporter Shera Dalin.

It happened again with *Contacts Connections Collaboration*. Bobbi was the perfect partner. She writes her own books and coaches others on how to write theirs. Her long career has provided many opportunities to bring people together in the creative arena, so she knew more about the topic then she realized. The secret ingredient in successful collaborations is chemistry. Writing a book with another person would be next to impossible without that "hot pink thread" that connects these co-authors. That is not something you can create; it just has to be there. And it is.

The subject of collaboration is a natural for Karen. Bringing it to the surface and making it real is what Bobbi does best. But there are a few other benefits as well. One is the friend-ship that has emerged from their professional collaboration (a bonus!). Another is the credibility factor for both authors in their separate fields of expertise. The third is the opportunity to introduce readers to a wide array of experts who would love to connect and collaborate with them. In addition, Karen says Bobbi is stuck with her forever! Their collaboration has only just begun.

What to look for in a collaborative relationship

A twenty-five-year veteran writer, **Sandra Beckwith** is the author of three books on publicity, a popular presenter at writers' conferences, and the developer of an e-course on book publicity. When she is considering a collaboration, she does her homework first. "I study how the person does business. Then, I engage with him to see how he interacts. Does he respond in a helpful way, or does he not respond at all? Is he friendly or distant?"

For Sandra, collaboration is about a willingness to share the load and be member of a team. "I think it helps if you approach your businesses in a similar way," she explains. "In fact, that's what I look for in a possible collaborator. I like somebody who wants to deliver more than what's expected and is committed to working hard to make the collaboration successful."

Not everyone lives up to those expectations. Some red flags are certain deal breakers. When a colleague wanted to rewrite Sandra's copyrighted online program, she declined because she couldn't be sure that the changes would be accurate, recommended, or ethical. Another friend agreed to write a guest blog to explain a specific process but then left out all the details because she "didn't want to give away her trade secrets."

"This is not a person I am likely to partner with on a project with income-generating potential," notes Sandra. "I like to work with people who are willing to share what they know."

How collaboration creates a win-win

When Sandra wanted to host a teleseminar for authors on how to use Goodreads for book promotion, she partnered with an expert on the Goodreads staff. "As a result," she says, "authors listening to the program found the session very valuable. Sharing this kind of information with authors is part of that Goodreads staffer's job description and bringing useful book marketing information to authors is part of mine. It was a win-win."

People want to do business with people they know, like, and trust. First, being connected means that you already know each other; second, if you do something or give something to another person, she will like you. Third, if you promise something and follow through, she will trust you. This is called a win-win. Finally, you may reciprocate. When someone does something nice for you, chances are, you will repay the favor by doing something nice for her.

As you get to know people you become interested in their goals and dreams and how you might be able help them by offering ideas, information, or introductions.

The Four "I"s of Collaboration

- Ideas

Ideas spark questions. What have you done so far? Have you thought of this? Do you know about that? Ideas can come quickly, and some people may become overwhelmed. Watch for nonverbal communication, such as body language, which will reveal this response. Others will be excited and respond immediately, grateful for your input and interest in them.

Ideas sometimes lead to unexpected collaborations. Karen's friend **Pat Adams** had an idea for an expo. At the time, she was the co-founder and publisher of a local newspaper, *Active Lifestyles.* Karen and Pat reached out to another newspaper publisher, Lucy Knapp. Lucy is the editor of the *St. Louis/St. Charles Women's Journal,* which publishes articles on topics of interest to women in the St. Louis and St. Charles metro area. Health and wellness are areas Lucy covers frequently.

This was an unlikely team, since technically, the two newspapers were competitors. "The plan was to have sponsors from outside the mall and to divide the proceeds after expenses in thirds," explains Pat. One really good feature of this collaboration is that Pat is very outgoing—a people person—while Lucy is more analytical and involved in writing and editing. "This expo would benefit both of our papers, as well as promote Gateway to Dreams," says Pat. "Karen has given so many people the opportunity to realize their dreams; this is one way to pay her back."

A few days before the expo, Karen, Pat, and Lucy hosted a meet and greet for exhibitors to get to know each other. The first Celebration of Women Expo was held in July 2015. It featured forty exhibitors and eighteen speakers and drew crowds all day. For the three organizers, it was a long but productive day. The expo's goal was to generate hundreds of connections for participants and attendees. It did just that, and it all began with an IDEA.

- **Information**

You may know of many different resources you can share (e.g., associations, books, articles, networking groups). If you share ideas in person, be sure to follow up with an email that spells out the details. That means you need to have the other person's business card. Make a note on the card or in your smart phone about what ideas or information you are sharing.

You never know where sharing information is going to lead. Sometimes, it leads to a life-long friendship and creative partnership, as is the case with Bobbi and marketing guru Bobette Kyle.

Bobbi met Bobette in 2004 at a St. Louis Publishers Association (SLPA) meeting. Bobette was on a panel about marketing and made an offer of a free workbook and a half hour of consulting. Bobbi signed on. The half hour of consulting lasted an hour; the ensuing friendship is still going strong.

That meeting was a turning point for Bobbi. "What do you really want to do?" Bobette asked her. "I want to be a ghostwriter," was the answer. And so began a new phase of Bobbi's career. The connection also manifested itself in helping Bobette move out of her office into a newly decorated home office, regular workout sessions, and a shared interest in SLPA.

But this association quickly became a dream team. Together, Bobbi and Bobette wrote the first iteration of Bobette's new website, myonlineweddinghelp.com; Bobette spoke to Bobbi's class on writing and publishing a nonfiction book; Bobbi edited Bobette's planner for women, *My Life Matters*; Bobette edited Bobbi's book, *Words To Live By*; Bobbi edited Bobette's ebook, *Dream Wedding On a Dime*; Bobette regularly rescues Bobbi from of her computer snafus; and every year they critique each other's marketing plans. In January 2014, they came full circle and (along with friend and favorite graphic designer Peggy Nehmen) participated in a panel discussion for SLPA.

- **Introductions**

Introduce two people to each other via email or Facebook. Include the reason you believe these two people should meet, some significant way that they can be of help to each other—not just because you're both from California or have brown hair. What is the strategic business reason? Karen always asks the person if he wants to be introduced. In this way, both parties are more open to the introduction. For example, if she knows someone who wants to write a book, she will ask Bobbi if she wants a referral. Then, she will suggest to the person that he should meet Bobbi. She will briefly outline Bobbi's background and send an email telling each person about the other. This way, both parties are "warmer"—more open—to meeting. Then, she backs out of it. The two people can take it from there.

Sometimes, introductions are more serendipitous. **Cynthia Correll** is the perfect example of what a chance encounter can lead to. Her life hasn't been the same, she says, since she met Karen at the *Small Business Monthly* Expo.

Cynthia was a virtual assistant with a background in graphic design. Since she moved to St. Louis from the West Coast, she has rebranded herself, expanded her business, and built an impressive roster of clients.

Karen invited Cynthia to attend several networking groups where she introduced her to what Cynthia calls "warm leads"—people who had already heard great things about her—and suggested several people to talk to. One person introduced her to another, who introduced her to someone else. "That started a chain of events that led to several new clients," Cynthia recalls. "Those people referred me to other people. I was meeting people I had never met before, and it got me back on track.

"One important outcome," says Cynthia, "was that people were seeing my creativity and hiring me to do more creative things. I moved into more right-brain activities that I had not fully recognized in myself." The first collaborative project Karen and Cynthia worked on was a redesign of the workbook for Joy of Goals, one of Karen's programs. This led to a project for a group called Experts for Entrepreneurs and a dream workbook for Gateway to Dreams. This was a group Cynthia could really relate to. She became very active and signed on as a Gateway to Dreams coach.

When **Peggy Nehmen** left her job at an advertising agency and went out on her own, her reputation for doing excellent work followed her. People who had worked with her in the past told other people, and she began to receive referrals. When her husband, Gary Kodner, decided to freelance as well, "it was like the flood gates burst open," Peggy recalls. "His friends called, and then those people went to other companies and hired him."

Someone who worked at Anheuser-Busch (AB) needed help with a magazine and was referred to Peggy. "We hit it off pretty well, and she gave me the name of somebody else at AB. We worked with him for a number of years. Then he went to another company and took us with him. Getting in the door at this new company was like a spider web. I have worked for several people there, so there's a lot of collaboration. They all know that I do a good job and call me for different projects. Then, somebody else will come out of the sky and say, 'Oh, hi. You know Katy. She told me to call you.' Or 'My colleague told me to reach out to you because we need help with a project.'"

Peggy's book-design projects began when she and Gary sold their studio on McCausland and were working out of their condo in Clayton. Peggy felt that she wasn't moving ahead fast enough and needed to network and meet people. "I had done a presentation at St. Louis Publishers Association a number of years ago," she says. "The membership fee was nominal, and I decided to join." Her first book, *Dressing Nifty After Fifty*, came about due to name recognition. "I knew Corrine Richardson, and Corrine knew someone I knew. She said, 'I want you to design my book.'

"I kept going to SLPA and working on their newsletter and meeting new people," says Peggy. "It has paid off. Every once in a while, somebody reached out to me because I had posted my name and a blurb about myself on the SLPA website. I have met people that way, and people have contacted me for book design. In a way, these were all referrals from SLPA because I didn't know them before they called."

Peggy's networking didn't end there. She goes to Meetups and other meetings; she takes part in an SLPA semi-annual workshop on self-publishing; she speaks to writing classes;

and she displays samples of her work at the SLPA Vendors' Showcase. What started as a decision to join one organization has helped her build a loyal following and a successful business.

- **Inspiration**

Sometimes what people need is to be re-inspired, re-motivated, reignited. Perhaps they are tired, overwhelmed, or burnt out. Maybe they don't feel up to the task or don't have anyone in their lives who understands their dream or their vision. What does it take to inspire someone? This is important to both Karen and Bobbi.

Karen loves to see people come alive, as opposed to sleepwalking. They need someone to be there for them, to give them encouragement, to be an example. By having conversations that inspire people, Karen thinks that they might see things in a different way. She wants to help people be seen, heard, loved, and supported—to feel hopeful. She listens on a deeper level and is very open to what her intuition tells her. Sometimes, she admits, she has to say something that makes people uncomfortable enough to take some action. If they're stuck in their stories, their stuff, their fears, they won't act. To make her point, she often advises, *"Don't let your story keep you stuck; let your possibilities set you free."*

Bobbi found herself in a position to motivate and inspire writers at the very beginning of her career. As a magazine editor, she was able to give new writers their first opportunity to see their words in print. Over the years, she found that being able to inspire creative people was one her greatest strengths.

As a book coach, it is a crucial skill. New authors need more than information; they need constant reinforcement and encouragement. Taking a book from the first glimmer of an idea to a tangible, finished product is a long journey. Every author, no matter how many books he may have written, needs a traveling companion.

The best kind of collaboration partner

Karen has a particular affinity for people who don't hide their hearts—who are open and genuine. She calls them "heart-smart" collaboration partners. You can recognize heart-smart people because they:

- Are more about loving people than judging people

- Care more about relationships than money

- Are deeply passionate about what they do

- Either know their purpose or are searching for their purpose

- Care less about being right than about how to work together

- Are committed to protecting and nurturing the planet

- Elicit a higher level of trust from others

- Accept people as they are

- Are exactly what they seem to be—transparent—without pretense

- Do not spend their time criticizing others

- Are respectful of others whose opinions may differ from their own

Six degrees of collaboration

The premise of six degrees of separation is that everyone in the world is connected to everyone else in the world by a chain of no more than six acquaintances. This theory was developed by Frigyes Karinthy in 1929, popularized by John Guare in his 1990 play of the same name, and turned into a parlor game called Six Degrees of Kevin Bacon.

In other words, we are all connected to everyone else by six friends of friends of friends. Says Tim Sanders, former chief solutions officer at Yahoo! "It really is an amazing principle; if truly embraced, it can help each of us understand that in the end, living life is about engaging in relationships and connecting with others. Everyone in our address book is a potential partner for someone else. Success in life is as simple as one contact away."

How to find people in your six-degrees-of-collaboration world

Sometimes, it's hard to avoid finding someone you know. Almost every conversation eventually leads to the question, "Oh, do you know so and so?" and if you participate in social media—especially Facebook—it's nearly impossible. Mark Zuckerberg's original intention was to connect people, and he succeeded on a grand scale by making it possible to see not only your friends but also mutual friends and your friends' friends.

Every time you log in, your world expands. To see what's happening with your friends' friends, just read their time-lines. When you mention someone in a post on Facebook, if you put an @ in front of her name, or type her name in bold, she will be notified that you mentioned her. LinkedIn always has a suggested list of "people you may know," and you can send them invitations to connect. If you do, Josh Turner and Karen suggest including a brief personal note instead of using the LinkedIn default invitation ("I'd like to connect with you on LinkedIn") because many people won't connect to someone they don't know. This next suggestion takes effort, but it produces results. After you connect online, turn that invitation into a strategic business connection by email or face-to-face introductions. Let people who know that you really want to know them, not just build a collection of names on LinkedIn.

Bill Prenatt has always understood the power of collaborative relationships. His ability to work with others to achieve business goals has played an important role in his corporate, small-business, and entrepreneurial career. One of his ventures, Experts for Entrepreneurs (e4e), is the result of a collaboration with Mason Duchatschek, a former colleague from his sales-management days. When Bill left the corporate world in 2008 to start his own business, he found it challenging at first to establish new connections. Mason was already a veteran entrepreneur when he and Bill launched e4e to help both of them grow their enterprises.

Like many small businesses, e4e altered its focus when necessary to meet the changing needs of its founders and the marketplace. Eventually, Mason left to pursue other goals, and Bill and his wife, Ann, took over the reins of the organization. Explains Bill, "E4e's purpose is help entrepreneurs and small business owners run and grow their businesses and live balanced lives. Most of the time, we see the need for change in random ways," says Bill. "E4e focuses on the use of systems as one vehicle to lead more productive and happier lives. E4e partners build relationships over a period of time that allow us to develop a deeper level of trust and be more receptive to learning from each other.

Each month, the twenty-five partners who have invested in e4e meet to share their knowledge and experience with each other and the guests who attend their meetings. Based on the model of TED Talks, three partners each give a fifteen-minute talk on running, growing, or living. The talks are tightly constructed and loaded with practical information. "A guest who pays $29 to attend an e4e meeting," says Bill, "comes away with $1,000 worth of value." Steven Denny has since taken the reins of e4e, and Bill continues to attend the meetings.

E4e is an example of collaboration not only on a grand scale but also at its best. When twenty-five people come together to share what they know for the benefit of all, their collective effort brings to life all of the definitions of collaboration at the beginning of this chapter:

- Working together to achieve a shared mission or goal

- Being an active member of the team

- Helping each other

- Harnessing the power of collective intelligence

- Creating synergy

- Brainstorming to solve a problem

- Building relationships

- Seeing the big picture

- Being inspired

- Leaving one's ego at the door

Conclusion

Of all the definitions of collaboration, this one seems to capture its meaning best: *harnessing the power of collective intelligence*. Creative people, intelligent people, capable people produce extraordinary results on their own. There has never been any doubt about that. Individual artists, writers, scientists, dancers—the list goes on and on—each create something uniquely his own. But, put two or more of those creative, intelligent, capable people together in pursuit of a common objective, and their combined output will take the creative process to an entirely new level.

Collaboration does more than add up the contributions of each member of a team; it multiplies them. A team brings several perspectives to any problem and diverse talents to any creative undertaking. That is the principle behind Broadway musical collaborations, ensemble movies and TV shows, and breakthrough business concepts (See Collaborations that made or changed history).

MEMORABLE QUOTES

"CREATING A BETTER WORLD requires teamwork, partnerships, and collaboration, as we need an entire army of companies to work together to build a better world within the next few decades. This means corporations must embrace the benefits of cooperating with one another." —*Simon Mainwaring*

"As you navigate through the rest of your life, be open to collaboration. Other people and other people's ideas are often better than your own. Find a group of people who challenge and inspire you, spend a lot of time with them, and it will change your life." —*Amy Poehler*

"We need to develop and disseminate an entirely new paradigm and practice of collaboration that supersedes the traditional silos that have divided governments, philanthropies, and private enterprises for decades and replace it with networks of partnerships working together to create a globally prosperous society." —*Simon Mainwaring*

"Collaboration is the best way to work. It's the only way to work, really. Everyone's there because they have a set of skills to offer across the board." —*Antony Starr*

"Life is not a solo act. It's a huge collaboration, and we all need to assemble around us the people who care about us and support us in times of strife." —*Tim Gunn*

"Most great advances have been a collaboration. That is the joy of science for me." —*Tim Hunt*

"Not being a genius, I believe in collaboration, and my background as a problem solver means I've never been afraid to work with people cleverer than myself." —*Daniel Barber*

"I have always believed in the power of collaboration ... If you don't collaborate, your ideas will be limited to your own abilities." —*Vishwas Chavan, Vishwasutras: Universal Principles for Living: Inspired by Real-Life Experiences*

"If we adopt the same collaborative mindset and practices that got to the moon and back, and that built the International Space Station, we can alleviate poverty—and do much more."— *Ron Garan, The Orbital Perspective: Lessons in Seeing the Big Picture from a Journey of 71 Million Miles*

"Collaboration is an inside-out mindset. It has to start on the inside, with the Heart." —*Jane Ripley, Collaboration Begins with You: Be a Silo Buster*

"I'm a proponent of collaboration ... Collaboration is valuable because it helps us transcend our individual limits and create something greater than ourselves." —*Bob Sullo*

"Training often gives people solutions to problems already solved. Collaboration addresses challenges no one has overcome before." —*Marcia Conner*

"Choose to collaborate (abundance perspective) and watch your competitors (scarcity perspective) become your allies." —*Jennifer Ritchie Payette*

"For collaboration to be effective, when we come together, we must put aside our interests and agendas and unite."—*J .A. Perez*

"Collaboration, it turns out, is not a gift from the gods but a skill that requires effort and practice." —*Douglas B. Reeves, Transforming Professional Development Into Student Results*

SYNERGY

"The whole is greater than the sum of its parts." —Aristotle
"Teamwork makes the dream work." —John Maxwell

———◆◇◆———

THIS CHAPTER IS ABOUT what happens when you bring contacts, connections, and collaboration together, how they create synergy, how the combination helps you and others achieve mutual goals and attain the unexpected benefits of connections and collaboration.

Defining synergy

The simplest explanation is, as Aristotle said, "The whole is greater than the sum of its parts" (1 + 1 = 5).

The more formal definition is, "The coordination of knowledge and effort of two or more people who work toward a definite purpose in the spirit of harmony." —Napoleon Hill

Synergy is what **Keith Sawyer, PhD**, calls group flow. "One of my professors, Mihaly Csikszentihalyi, published a book called *Flow: The Psychology of Optimal Experience*," recalls Sawyer. "Group flow is when a group collectively gets into a state of peak performance. This is the highest level of group performance. The scientific term is *emergence* or *collaborative emergence*."

Sawyer is a jazz pianist and plays piano for the Chicago Improvisational Theater Group. He is fascinated with how such ensembles create fully coherent, humorous stage plays without a script. "Jazz and improv groups have the philosophy that the whole is greater than the sum of its parts," he explains. "What they produce is something unpredictable and unplanned—something no member of the group could have produced alone."

How synergy develops

- **Alone**: When you try to do things by yourself, you are limited. While there is the potential for creativity, it is up to you to create it on your own.

- **Contacts**: There is magic, but you can't see it. It's just a seed, not yet apparent.

- **Connection**: You can almost see the beginning of the magic. You can sense the potential even if you can't define it.

- **Collaboration**: The magic has begun as you work with others to reach a common goal.

- **Synergy**: This is collaboration at a higher level.

When Peggy and Bobbi work together, what matters are the client and the book. What can they do together to make a book more than it could be with either of them working on their parts separately?

The difference between collaboration and synergy

- Collaboration is a process; synergy is alive, organic, more than a process.

- Synergy involves trust; when it is being created, people are bringing something higher to the relationship. The question is not "What we are going to gain?" but rather "What can we create?"

- Synergy involves a mission that is bigger than the participants. It's not a goal; it's a mission.

- In collaboration, people work together to achieve a purpose; in synergy, they combine like chemical elements, to create something new.

- Collaboration ignites the spark; synergy is the fire.

- Synergy triggers passion, power, and possibilities.

- Synergy is more than words or intentions. It has a life of its own; it is a separate entity.

- Something real is being created. It has form.

- Synergy goes beyond connection and collaboration; it is a relationship, full of positivity, full of potential.

- "No two minds ever come together without thereby creating a third invisible, intangible force, which may be likened to a third mind." —Napoleon Hill

- "Going beyond collaboration is combining the unique strengths of each individual to create something greater than the whole. This fusion of specialized skills and abilities is the key to the magic." —Bobette Kyle

- When we appreciate the others with whom we are working, we acknowledge them for what they're bringing to the table.

- Synergy can do so much more and go so much further than mere collaboration.

Synergy at work

If several countries get together to accomplish something, they are collaborating. But if the United Nations gets behind the effort, the collective power of all of those countries is synergy. When that happens, things get done.

When Karen and Cynthia work together, both get far more out of everything they do. Karen feels free to be exactly who she is, without apology, and Cynthia "gets" her. When they work together, their brainstorming produces far greater results.

Bobbi works hand-in-hand with Peggy Nehmen, of Nehmen-Kodner Graphic Design, to produce professionally edited, beautifully designed books. Their creative collaboration has evolved and grown over the years to become a perfect partnership. The third critical member of their team is always the book's author. Each one contributes something special to the mix: the concept and the content, the skills to refine and polish the prose, and the talent to bring it to life, visually. There is no better example of synergy than the book that results from their combined efforts.

Let's use Gateway to Dreams as another example of how contacts lead to connections, which lead to collaboration, which—*when the stars align perfectly*—leads to synergy. Karen had a dream: To encourage people to believe in *their* dreams. But she wanted to take it one step further by building a support system for each dreamer—a group of people who would also believe in believe in and support the dreams of others.

Creating a community

To make Gateway to Dreams real, Karen had to convince others to join her in figuring out how to make it happen. She invited some of her connections, and they invited some of theirs; and soon a community was born. It met every week to brainstorm about how to turn this dream into a reality. Members of this group had a focus that bound them together and fused their energy. They had a storefront space in Chesterfield Mall, painted and furnished it (with gifts from many generous people who also believed in this dream), and on January 10, 2014, Gateway to Dreams opened its doors.

- **Dream Tank**

Once Gateway had a physical location, the next step was the creation of a program called the Dream Tank, which provides an opportunity for people to come together and share their dreams. The format is simple: Attendees break up into small groups of five, with a facilitator/coach at each table. Each person shares something he or she wants to achieve, have, do, or be; and others at the table ask questions and make suggestions. The key is that each person leaves with one action item to work on during the upcoming week. The facilitator checks in during the week to see what progress has been made and offer encouragement.

- **Other new programs**

Gateway has created two more programs: The Business Lodge for Women and Connecting & Promoting Women (CPW). The Business Lodge is a 6400-square-foot co-working space in West St. Louis County, Missouri, which focuses on helping entrepreneurs work with experts on their businesses and connect with coaches and experts. CPW is a networking program established to build membership and sponsorships, as well as to promote Gateway to Dreams to the larger community. What sets CPW apart are its openness to everyone, many opportunities for networking, and educational programs. At each meeting, two speakers give short presentations on various business and life topics.

These are the current Gateway to Dreams programs, but there may well be more to come in the future. The overarching goal of all of them is not only to help people achieve their own dreams but also to find ways to help others achieve theirs. According to Karen, "All of these programs are about bringing people together to get to know each other and discover the depth of knowledge and talent that may not be immediately apparent when they first meet. When you meet someone new," she says, "you never know if that person is exactly the right person at the right time or if she knows someone else you should meet."

What true synergy looks like

We could fill many more pages with theories and examples of what true collaboration can lead to. But nothing is more powerful than a true story. Bobbi's friend, client, and coach, Joe Sherrer, has shared a remarkable story of synergy in action. This story captures everything required for synergy to occur, from the elements that must be present to what they look like when they come together. What is even more amazing is how Joe has somehow managed to encapsulate the message of contacts, connections, and collaboration and gift-wrap it for all of us.

Joe Sherrer was twenty-one when he entered the Air Force and took a communications-engineering program on how to practice engineering "the Air Force way." In his class were twelve other young officers who did not know each other when they arrived. They were in Joe's words, "contacts," of which he would make thousands more over the course of his career. What made them special and helped to forge an instant connection was that they were all wearing the uniform. There was one person in particular named Tony with whom Joe developed a close friendship, but when the course ended, they went their separate ways.

"Fast-forward almost twenty years," says Joe. "Tony and I were both at the Pentagon, when some countries that weren't exactly friendly to the United States had figured out how to break into the Department of Defense (DOD) leadership emails. Secretary of Defense Donald Rumsfeld was not happy about this. As the technical remediation took place to repair the damage, a larger strategic discussion ensued about the threat to DOD networks.

"As a result of this debate, I was asked to 'think strategically' about how to respond. Not long after, I proposed to my Marine three-star boss in charge of cyber security that we needed a well-reasoned military strategy to align the DOD around a set of principles to deal with the threat (we didn't have one at the time). He took the idea to the chairman of the Joint Chiefs of Staff, General Peter Pace, who immediately approved it.

"I was a lieutenant colonel at the time and was asked to develop and write the first national military strategy for cyberspace operations that provided an integrated approach to improve both defense of DOD networks and our ability to take offensive action against our adversaries, *if necessary, through cyberspace*. This was the first time that kind of strategic thinking had ever really been seriously dealt with in such a comprehensive way by our military leadership."

Joe's orders were to form his team. The first person he picked was Tony, the friend he had gone to school with twenty years earlier. "We knew each other inside out. There was this absolute trust; it was almost as if I could say something, and he would finish the sentence. There were four others from that course who I knew were working in various other positions and deployments in the Air Force. I picked them as well because there was that same kind of trust. It was more than a connection; it went beyond collaboration.

"Because of the chemistry and dynamics, the urgency of the job, and the support we were getting, all of us came together in such a magnificent way from start to finish. We not only wrote the strategy, we also coordinated it across all four military departments, approximately fifty-two DOD agencies, the Department of Homeland Security, the National Security Council, and parts of the intelligence community. And we did that in *fifteen months,* which was nothing short of a minor miracle. There was a point where things were happening automatically because we all knew what each of us needed to do on that particular day in order to keep moving the effort forward.

"There was 100 percent commitment to the task and a sense that we were going to do this together. Everybody was respected; everybody was making his own contribution, no matter how small or large; everybody was appreciated. Events like this are very, very rare. I could count them on one hand when I was in the service."

Joe deployed four times while he was in the service. In the field, he explains, you rely on people you already know have gone through similar experiences and whom you trust. Shared history and a shared purpose develop, creating a team. As part of a team, people are more resilient, they are more committed, and their talents come together in such a way that the results are greater than the sum of the parts.

"A team can't be just a bunch of contacts; a team can't just be a bunch of connections; a team goes far beyond those first two steps to collaboration. A team—a true team, like the one I described when I was at the Pentagon—takes collaboration to a whole other level: *synergy*. As a result, it is able to do more and achieve more."

The synergy of a great team is the end result of several hard-to-come-by elements: a shared purpose, in which everybody understands what they are doing and why; a shared commitment in which people are psychologically invested in the outcome and in each other; and shared trust and the ability to work through the interpersonal challenges that inevitably come up.

"With shared purpose, shared commitment, and shared trust you have the makings of something very, very special," says Joe Sherrer, and he is in a position to know.

Conclusion

The word synergy has multiple meanings. Dictionaries and thesauri define it as "cooperative interaction, cooperation, combined effort, give and take." It's also a trendy business term. Corporations merge and announce that, by eliminating overlapping functions and positions, they have achieved "synergies." That is not the definition on which this chapter is based. Rather, it was intended to reflect the way Napoleon Hill understood the meaning of the word.

We see synergy as the best possible outcome of a process that begins with a simple contact with someone new. It doesn't matter how this contact comes about—at a networking event, through an introduction, or just by chance. One never knows where it may lead. In the best of all possible worlds, it leads to a real connection with that person, and then to a collaborative project, and finally to results that are far beyond what either person could have accomplished alone.

MEMORABLE QUOTES

"TOGETHER WE ARE STRONGER, our voices louder, and the synergy of our actions more powerful." —*Pierce Brosnan*

"When it all boils down, it's about embracing each other's stories and maybe even finding that synergy to collaborate for the common good." —*Dhani Jones*

"Servant leadership is the foundation and the secret of Sam Walton's ability to achieve team synergy."—*Michael Bergdahl*

"Synergy is what happens when one plus one equals ten or a hundred or even a thousand! It's the profound result when two or more respectful human beings determine to go beyond their preconceived ideas to meet a great challenge." —*Stephen Covey*

"Synergy and serendipity often play a big part in medical and scientific advances." —*Julie Bishop*

"Synergy between thoughts and feelings reads the universe like an opened book." —Toba Beta, My Ancestor Was an Ancient Astronaut

"The greatest benefit of synergy is born in the diversity of perspectives. The highest value can be found in these variances. Too much of the same does not create change in the same way." —*Danielle Marie Crune*

"Talent wins games, but teamwork and intelligence win championships." —*Michael Jordan*

"Never doubt that a small group of thoughtful, committed people can change the world. Indeed, it is the only thing that ever has." —*Margaret Mead*

"No one can whistle a symphony. It takes an orchestra to play it." —*H.E. Luccock*

"We have no choice but to think together, ponder together, in groups and communities. The question is how to do this, how to come together and think and hear each other in order to touch, and be touched by, the intelligence we need." —*Jacob Needleman.*

CONNECTION DURING CRISES

"Yet, taught by time, my heart has learned to glow for other's good, and melt at other's woe." —Homer

—◦—

THE PANDEMIC THAT STEAMROLLED our lives in 2020 and continues to affect what our *new* normal might be, has given us the gift of perspective. Because connection and relationships are more challenging than ever, we have realized the struggle that comes with facing crises—no matter how widespread they are felt—is simply a part of life. Regardless of what you're facing, relationships can be what that get you through tough times.

When Tragedy Strikes

Rosemary Britts is the executive director and founder of the Sickle Cell Association (SCA). Through SCA she and her staff provide services and education to families dealing with the disease as well as providing awareness to the public, advocating for policy change to better aid families who continue to cope with Sickle Cell Disease. For twenty-eight years, Rosemary had been a mom and caretaker to her daughter, the inspiration for her work with the Sickle Cell community.

On September 23, 2019, after speaking at an event as a Sickle Cell advocate, Rosemary got a heartbreaking call she was not expecting. While her daughter was in the emergency room seeking relief from pain, a common occurrence for anyone with Sickle Cell, healthcare workers were unable to help.

"Mom," she had told Rosemary, "You can go home. And I'll call you when I'm ready to be picked up." That phone call never came.

Her daughter had been born with the disease, so Rosemary knew firsthand what other individuals and families were dealing with. From 2011 when she founded SCA to 2019, Rosemary felt like she had purpose, but on that September day, her whole world changed.

Quitting wasn't an option.

"Mom," she could imagine her daughter saying, "you still have something to offer people and continue on the road that you've been traveling. You can still help others with this dreadful disease through our experiences."

On a basic level, that's where Rosemary continues to get her strength to this day. But her trials weren't over. After the pandemic swept through the world in 2020, only seven months after losing her daughter, Rosemary also lost her greatest ally when her husband became a victim to COVID-19.

Still dealing with the deep grief surrounding the loss of her daughter and husband, she continued trying to help other people at a time when her main warriors had gone on.

"My husband has been my rock, my supporter in every way," she shared. But because her organization is a non-profit, her fundraising efforts were always used to help others. Without a partner's income to sustain her, Rosemary was faced with difficult decisions. "I felt as if I was struck by lightning twice."

But Rosemary knew she was called to stay the course. After things had shut down due to COVID restrictions, she had to get creative. Clients were still in need of services and even more so due to loss of jobs, supplemental income, and in some cases, people. So, a dress up tea party SCA had hosted in the past which brought in their biggest donors was transitioned into a virtual event. People jumped right in, dressed up, shared with friends and family, and even brought their own tea sets to the virtual party.

Knowing that our world as we knew it had shifted, Rosemary made a plan. The association also hosted virtual walks, sold t-shirts, and created online educational workshops to continue their work educating others about Sickle Cell.

"You have to let people know what's going on in order for them to know how to help you," Rosemary expressed. "Staying connected with clients because they still have needs even if they're afraid to reach out to me, realizing that I'm going through my own time of need, is so important to me. I'm here for them, but I'm also here for myself. This is the work I'm meant to do, and staying connected, asking for help, and keeping my eye on the work God has called me to is how I get through."

You can support the Sickle Cell community by becoming a blood donor. To support Rosemary's work, please check out www.sicklecellassociation.org.

The Heartbreak of Divorce

Precious Smith's experience with crisis is perhaps one of the more relatable topics of our shared human experience: divorce. When she got get married in January of 2012, she would have never imagined a divorce by 2014.

Precious is someone with a strong faith system and background. After meeting some individuals in college who talked to her about finding her way to a personal spiritual foundation, she continued to grow her faith through the years. In December 2009, she was in a church service where a very powerful woman told her that the Lord had someone hand-picked for her.

"I come from a background where marriage is something that wasn't glorified; it wasn't something that was always talked about. I grew up watching my mom in an abusive marriage and I wasn't interested. Everyone in my background had a lot of kids, and there were no male figures."

Over the holidays in 2009-2010, Precious was visiting her sister who kept talking to her about a gentleman who lived next door. He went to church and was kind. In Precious' mind, she was just grateful that her family was living next to a nice guy. But then she had a chance to meet him, spend time with him, and a relationship ensued. It wasn't all peaches and cream. In fact, they went to counseling while dating, broke up a couple of times, then finally decided on marriage. The red flags she had seen would be ignored. For a little while, at least.

Six months into the marriage, she knew they were in trouble. When Precious would want to talk about her feelings, desires, and tried to connect with her husband, she wouldn't have his participation. One day, he simply stated, "I have no desire for this anymore."

It was a hurt impossible to understand unless you've been in her shoes. "Give me a reason!" Precious wanted to demand. "Cheat on me, let me attack your character, but don't let this all be about not wanting *me!*"

She was fighting to avoid rejection, throwing herself into fix-it mode. Insisting on counseling, trying to compel him to talk it through, and demanding they should be fighting for each other.

"I was showing up, I wasn't cheating. I was a good wife," she recalls. "I'm a communicator, but because he wasn't, I would almost walk on eggshells. I felt like he would want me more if I just remained quiet. And so, I started getting quiet. I didn't speak up anymore in the house."

After he left, Precious was in the habit of silencing herself, not fully knowing who she was anymore. She had gone to her pastoral leaders, but she had yet to heal on the inside.

The final blow was when he declared: "We're going to go our separate ways."

She sat in church pews hurting, broken, and wondering why this happened to her. There was so much shame and embarrassment to cope with. Precious considered herself to be the first one in her family to get the promise of a healthy long-term relationship when suddenly, it was taken away. It became difficult to be around people because she began to feel as if no one wanted to be around her. She even deleted her social media accounts for four and a half years.

"I knew I had to get some help for what I was dealing with. I was showing up, but I wasn't myself."

The connections and support system she had built was invaluable through crisis. Her friends would pray with her, help her with the day-to-day of life, a friend even moved in with her, and she began picking up the pieces.

"I'm ready to forgive," she said one morning. After not being able to emotionally handle seeing her ex on the street, Precious began to forgive. By helping others with her story, she saw relationships experience growth and healing.

"I learned that sometimes that you get healed by helping other people if you are going through a tough time. I never imagined that having a failed marriage would help another marriages avoid failure, but I began to see miracles when I connected with people."

Precious knows that her story would be different without the investment others made in her. Listening to motivational speakers like Les Brown and reading personal development books were a huge part of her healing. She is now a coach for others.

"When you know who you are, it will overflow into your business, it will overflow into your relationships. So, during hard times, invest in yourself, pull back and reread, recalibrate, reconfigure so you can return to the real world and touch people in a different way. Whether that's in business, in relationship, or any other part of life," Precious advises.

Coping With A Worldwide Pandemic

Though the world has seen pandemics, wars, endemics and the like, the scale of COVID-19 in the Age of Information has affected humanity in new ways. We hope to learn from them all. After a couple years of lockdowns, losses, and major shifts in our world, we asked a few respected leaders to weigh in on their experience.

Mason Duchatschek, Bestselling Author and Speaker

How has your business changed during crises?

"Since many of my clients operate in states that were shut down (and many are still) my revenue plummeted, and it was totally out of my control. So, I focused my efforts on things within my power that I could do. I wrote and published, three books. I also built my network on LinkedIn and offered copies of my books to people I wanted to initiate a relationship with if they agreed to connect. Bottom Line: I did not waste time. I expanded my network and added value to the people in it."

What solutions have you found to help you grow and adapt?

"Focusing on things I *could* do instead of the things I could not do, change or fix."

What is the best business advice you have ever received concerning building relationships while coping with crisis or change?

"Become the person who attracts the type of people and opportunities that will expand and enhance both my personal and professional life. It requires a continual focus on improvement, courage beyond comfort zones, and relentless forward progress and follow through."

Bill Prenatt, Simply Successful

How has your business changed during crises?

"I view challenges, including the COVID-19 pandemic, as an opportunity to explore new ways to serve my clients."

What solutions have you found to help you grow and adapt?

"Think more. React less."

What is the best business advice you have ever received concerning building relationships while coping with crisis or change?

"Recognizing that none of what we do is new and just building on what is already been done is the most effective way to get things done."

Cathy Sexton, Strategist and Coach

How has your business changed during crises?

"I lost a few clients, some clients are booming while others...not so much. This period has given me the time to work on my online programs which I have been able to launch. I have also had time to reflect on the direction of my business. I was already working towards trying to create a 99% virtual format and this situation has made that much easier to accomplish."

What solutions have you found to help you grow and adapt?

"Embracing and using the technology that I already had like zoom, and my online course software. Revisiting programs I have already invested in and investing in new programs."

What is the best business advice you have ever received concerning building relationships while coping with crisis or change?

"I know this sounds easy to say, and much harder to do, but is so worth it. Remembering, "one day at a time, staying true to self, and being transparent with what was going on in my life, are not just cliches. By living all of those fully, I was able to still run a business and live life, deal with a very ill daughter, losing two dear friends, and the love of my life all in a short couple years. Not that it was easy but so thankfully I learned to take one day at a time, deal with how you feel and be grateful for every day, minute and friend you have."

Karen Hoffman, Gateway To Dreams

How has your business changed during crises?

"Our nonprofit was built around in-person meetings and events. During the outbreak of COVID-19 in the US during the spring of 2020, we immediately stopped all face-to-face meetings, thinking in a few months we would resume. That was obviously not the case. So our biggest "change" was when we could no longer be around each other.

What solutions have you found to help you grow and adapt?

"I was shocked that a platform I previously had been very vocal about not liking, became our best friend. I believe we would have had a much harder time sustaining members without the video platform, Zoom. I previously preferred conference calls because I was familiar with them, and fought using new online video services. However, our nonprofit is relationship-based, full of supportive members–primarily women–and Zoom has given us that much-needed interaction that *almost* feels physical. We can SEE each other. We can notice moods. We can HEAR each other more fully when we get to interact visibly. We have literally had members in thankful tears because they missed the human interaction and community that was closed to us all."

Debbie Champion, Attorney

How has your business changed during crises?

"Some changes we have seen is that court's were closed, people were not meeting in person but via Zoom, but we have been busier with client calls, retentions, meetings, and calls with attorneys. My email receipts have gone from an average of 300 a day (which was already too high) to 400 a day. My appointments have doubled. I cannot tell whether the stress level of lawyers has increased because of COVID or because of the increase in responsibilities during the pandemic!"

What solutions have you found to help you grow and adapt?

"We have hired associates, secretaries, a new office manager, and clerks, to help us through this massive influx. I did not think that would happen during a pandemic, but for my business it did. Getting the support I needed through this time is the solution that worked for me."

What is the best business advice you have ever received concerning building relationships while coping with crisis or change?

"My best advice is: don't be absent. If you are not hearing from people, call them. Realize they might be less flexible than you, more overwhelmed. And if you are there to help, you continue to receive their trust and their reliance, and hopefully, their business. When I have had down time during this period, I have sent notes or cards of emails just telling people I am thinking of them and cannot wait to see them in person, or to have lunch or whatever we would have been doing differently during normal times. It has made a big difference. And as always, if you want more business. *Pick up the phone!"*

Aubrey Betz, District Manager

How has your business changed during crises?

I don't own a business, but I work for an organization. I would say there's a struggle to connect with people. That's the biggest change. Finding ways to connect without getting too close or seeing full faces.

What solutions have you found to help you grow and adapt?

I've heard a lot of people talking about 'smizing' – or smiling with your eyes. I think more than ever it's important to show empathy. That's become a buzz word, but truly showing someone you've heard what they said and understand is invaluable.

What is the best business advice you have ever received concerning building relationships while coping with crisis or change?

Validation. It's similar to empathy, but not many people know how to use it. So often when someone is speaking, we are thinking about what to say next. But by validating what someone said and confirming that you understand or it's ok to feel/think that way, you are showing them you heard. There's also so much that's hinted at, but never truly said out loud. So when you become more adept at listening you start to pick up on those things and pull them out for more discussion.

Maxine Clark, Build-A-Bear

How has your business changed during crises?

"Our biggest foundation project was heating up just as COVID quarantine started. Blueprint4Summer.com had to switch gears to support camps and the idea of virtual camp. We were able to put time and talent together to help our camps have a successful summer!"

What solutions have you found to help you grow and adapt?

"I have loved the opportunity to learn. I have been able to attend many events all across the country that I would not have been able to travel to. It has been for me, a time to thrive."

What is the best business advice you have ever received concerning building relationships while coping with crisis or change?

"Look on the sunny side of every problem. That is where the opportunity is shining bright!"

MEMORABLE QUOTES

—◆◇◆—

"I<small>T IS AN ABSOLUTE</small> human certainty that no one can know his own beauty or perceive a sense of his own worth until it has been
reflected back to him in the mirror of another loving, caring human being." —*John Joseph Powell*

"We cannot live only for ourselves. A thousand fibers connect us with our fellow men; and among those fibers, as sympathetic threads, our actions run as causes, and they come back to us as effects." —*Herman Melville*

"Sometimes, reaching out and taking someone's hand is the beginning of a journey. At other times, it is allowing another to take yours." —*Vera Nazarian*

"No one has ever become poor by giving."—*Anne Frank*

"The best way to not feel hopeless is to get up and do something. Don't wait for good things to happen to you. If you go out and make some good things happen, you will fill the world with hope, you will fill yourself with hope."—*Barack Obama*

"No one is useless in this world who lightens the burdens of another." —*Charles Dickens*

"A kind gesture can reach a wound that only compassion can heal." —*Steve Maraboli*

"One of the most important things you can do on this earth is to let people know they are not alone." —*Shannon L. Alder*

"When we give cheerfully and accept gratefully, everyone is blessed."—*Maya Angelou*

RESOURCES

Contributors to this book

- Pat Adams
  Gateway to Dreams volunteer
  adamspatriciah@gmail.com

- Bob Baker
  Author of *Guerrilla Music Marketing* books
  Founder of the Empowered Artist Movement
  http://www.bob-baker.com
  bob@bob-baker.com

- Sandra Beckwith
  Build Book Buzz
  Beckwith Communications
  25 Erie Crescent
  Fairport, NY 14450
  585-377-2768

http://buildbookbuzz.com/

- Beth Thater Maune
  Pleaidian Dignitary
  Unlock Your Soul's
  Purpose
  1-636-299-8694
  beththater@me.com
  www.UnlockYourSoulsPurpose.com

- Aubrey Betz
  Blogger, Free Coffee With Aubrey
  www.freecoffeewithaubrey.com

- Don Breckenridge, Jr.
  CEO and Co-founder Hatchbuck
  (314) 288-0399 Ex. 101
  dbreckenridge@hatchbuck.com
  www.Hatchbuck.com

- Debbie Champion Rynearson
  Suess Schnurbusch & Champion, LLC
  500 N. Broadway, Suite 1550
  St. Louis, MO 63102
  314-421-4430
  dchampion@rssclaw.com
  http://www.rssclaw.com

- Arlen Chalef
  314-994-7784

314-369-0746

- Maxine Clark
  Founder, Build A Bear
  maxine@clark-fox.com

- Cynthia Correll
  Communications Architect
  www.CynthiaCorrell.com

- Mason Duchatschek
  #1 Best-selling
  Author, Keynote Speaker, and Entrepreneur
  Co-author of *Attract, Capture & Convert,*
  Defeating an Internet Boogeyman, and *Sales Utopia*
  www.Buildatribe.com
  www.MasonDuchatschek.com
  www.BusinessWebVideos.com
  masonduke@gmail.com

- Lori Feldman
  314-485-4350
  diva@thedatabaseiva.com
  http://www.thedatabasediva.com

- Karen Cain Fox
  636-677-7654
  314-323-5493
  karen@karentheconnector.com
  http://karentheconnector.com

- Felicia Graber, Author of *Amazing Journey: Metamorphosis of a Hidden Child*
  Co-author of *Our Father's Voice: A Holocaust Memoir*
  feliciagraber@earthlink.net

- Will Hanke
  Founder & Owner Red Canoe Media
  314-514-5736
  will@redcanoemedia.com
  http://www.redcanoemedia.com

- Laura Herring, MA, CRP, GMS
  Founder and Chairwoman, Impact Group
  Author of *No Fear Allowed: A Story of Guts, Perseverance, and Making an Impact.*
  http://www.nofearallowed.com

- Lucy Knapp
  St. Louis Women's Journals
  314-803-6777
  Lucy@womens-journals.com
  Lucyknapp314@gmail.com
  http://www.womens-journals.com

- Mary Kutheis
  mary@realcontentment.com
  http://www.realcontentment.com

- Bobette Kyle
  MyOnlineWeddingHelp

bobette@myonlineweddinghelp.com
http://www.MyOnlineWeddingHelp.com
http://www.AspirationalBride.com/

* Peggy Nehmen, Co-founder & Partner
Nehman-Kodner Creative
12452 New Wooding Ct.
St. Louis, MO 63146
314-548-6001
pnhmen@gmail.com
http://www.n-kcreative.com

* Lethia Owens, Personal Branding Strategist
314-517-6201
http://lethiaowens.com/
lethia@lethiaowens.com

* Bill Prenatt, Simply Successful
Experts4Entrepreneurs
P.O. Box 6130
Chesterfield, MO 63006
bill.prenatt@simplysuccessful-llc.com
http://simplysuccessful-llc.com

* Keith Sawyer, PhD
Morgan Distinguished Professor in Educational In-
novations
University of North Carolina at Chapel Hill
Campus Box 3500 Chapel Hill, NC 27599
www.keithsawyer.com

keithsawyer.wordpress.com
@drkeithsawyer

- Cathy Sexton, Strategist & Coach
  The Productivity Experts
  65 Guylyn Place
  Valley Park, MO 63088
  cathy@TheProductivityExperts.com
  http://www.TheProductivityExperts.com

- Josh Turner
  LinkedSelling
  314-499-8892
  josh@linkedselling.com
  http://www.linkedselling.com

- Marcia Layton Turner
  Ghostwriter and executive director
  Association of Ghostwriters
  marcia@associationofghostwriters.org
  http://www.associationofghostwriters.org

- Jane Ubell-Meyer
  Madison & Mulholland, Inc.
  917 848 3353
  jane@madisonandmulholland.com
  http://www.madisonandmulholland.com

- Glenda Woolley
  5 Star Leadership, LLC

glenda@5starleadership.com

http://www. 5starleadership.com

* Kim Wolterman

  314-968-8293

  314-283-4605

  Author of *Who's Been Sleeping in My Bed(room)? Researching a St. Louis County, Missouri Home ;*
  Keys to Unlocking House History; From Buckeye to G.I.

  Leroy C. Kubler the War Years,1942-1945
  kimwolterman@gmail.com

Networking Groups

  * **eWomen network**

H TTP://WWW.EWOMENNETWORK.COM

  Business Network International(BNI)

http://www.bni.com/
  * **Company of Friends**

http://www.fastcompany.com/cof/index.jsp
  * **CoolTea**

http://www.pj2.com/cooltea/
  * **Ecademy**

http://www.ecademy.com/
  * **ItsNotWhatYouKnow**

http://www.forbes.com/fdc/welcome_mjx.shtml

National Networking Groups and Resource Associations

- **Netparty**

http://www.netparty.com

- **Networking for Professionals**

http://www.networkingforprofessionals.com

- **Point Relevance**

http://www.pointrelevance.com

- **PowermingleMingleZone™ and PowerminglegleNetwork™**

http://www.powermingle.com/

- **Toastmasters International**

http://www.toastmasters.org/

- **U.S. Jaycees**

http://www.usjaycees.org/main.htm

- **Google Groups**

Books and Audio CDs

- Collaborative Intelligence: Thinking with People

Who Think Differently by Dawna Markova and Angie McArthur

- How Full Is Your Bucket? by Tom Rath and Don Clifton

- Life is a Verb: 37 Days to Wake Up, Be Mindful, and Live Intentionally by Patti Digh

- Love Is the Killer App: How to Win Business and Influence Friends by Tim Sanders and Gene Stone

- Relationship Networking: The Art of Turning Contacts Into Connections by Sandra Yancey

- Swim With the Sharks by Harvey Mackay

- Little Black Book of Connections: 6.5 Ways for Networking Your Way to Rich Relationships by Jeffrey Gitomer

- The 7 Levels of Communication byMichael Maher

- TheHeart and Art of Netweaving: Building Meaningful Relationships One Connection at a Time by Robert Littell

- People Hire People, Not Resumes by Frank Danzo

- The Tipping Point by Malcolm Gladwell

- The Go Giver by Bob Burg

- You Were Born For This by Bruce Wilkinson

- Pay It Forward by Kathryn Ryan Hyde

- How to Fly a Horse: The Secret History of Creation, Invention, and Discovery by Kevin Ashton

- The Innovators: How a Group of Hackers, Geniuses, and Geeks Created the Digital Revolution by Walter Isaacson

- Where Good Ideas Come From by Steven Johnson

Business-Building Membership Organizations

- Bill Prenatt – Experts 4 Entrepreneurs http://www.e4ecommunity.com

- Karen Hoffman – Gateway to Dreams http://www.gatewaytodreams.org

Connecting With Media

- NichePower Media Guide Connect with more than 200 local media and grow your business;145 print publications, 50 radio stations, 8 TV stations

Customer Relationship Management Systems

- Benchmark One (CRM & email program combined): http://www.benchmarkone.com

- Microsoft Outlook http://office.microsoft.com/en-u s/outlook/

- Insightly (CRM) http://www.insightly.com/

- Goldmine http://techsell.net/GoldMine/

- Nimble https://app.nimble.com/

Database Management

- Lori Feldman – ACT! Database classes and training http://www.thedatabasediva.com

- Amy Porterfield – (Drip campaigns, list building) http://www.amyporterfield.com/

- Daniel Rubinstein – converts business cards to lists (Scans leads and delivers a spreadsheet) http://www.cards2list.com

Email Marketing

- Swift Page - http://www.swiftpage.com

- AWeber - http://www.aweber.com/

- Market Volt - http://www.marketvolt.com

- Constant Contact - http://www.ConstantContact.com

- MailChimp- http://www.mailchimp.com

- Vista Print (Free or inexpensive marketing tools) -http://www.vistaprint.com Get-connected-stay-connected kit

- Sterilite small clip box dimensions: 11x6, 5/8 x 2-3/4 Need help finding a product? Call 1-800-295-5510

- "Really Useful Box" from Really Useful Products, Ltd. Size is 1.7 litre US patent 7159733 http://www.officedepot.com/a/products/452333/Really-Useful-Boxes-Plastic-Storage-Box/

- Post-it® notes (2x1.5) http://www.postit.com/wps/portal/3M/en_US/PostItNA/Home?WT.mc_id=www.Post-it.com

- Business cards

- Pens

- Snack-size sandwich bags

Top 10 Social Networking Sites

- Facebook http://www.facebook.com

- Twitter http://www.twitter.com

- Google+ https://plus.google.com/

- YouTube https://www.youtube.com/

- LinkedIn https://www.linkedin.com/

- Instagram http://instagram.com/

- Periscope https://www.periscope.tv/

- Pinterest http://www.pinterest.com

- Snapchat https://www.snapchat.com/

- TikTok https://www.tiktok.com/

ABOUT THE AUTHORS

 Karen S. Hoffman is the founder of Gateway to Dreams, a non-profit community of dreamers and dream champions, and City of Experts, which connects expert speakers, authors, consultants, and coaches with people who need their expertise. Karen spent twenty years in the barter industry and, along with co-author, Shera Dalin, wrote *The Art of Barter –How to Trade for Almost Anything.*

Karen is dedicated to encouraging dreamers and promoting and connecting business owners. An extreme multiprenuer, she is a former magazine owner and publisher and the creator of the *NichePower Media Guide*. She is also the guiding force behind the Joy of Goals workshops, Dream Tank, Connecting & Promoting Women, The Business Lodge (a collaborative work space for women), and Your Collaborative Board.

Recognized in 2007 as the Business MatchMaker of the Year by eWomen Network, Karen is a recipient of the Regional Chamber's Business Pacesetter Award, as well as the Small Business Administration's Home-Based Business Champion of the Year for region IV.

Still married and in love with her high school sweetheart, Rick, Karen is the proud mother of Mitzi, Jaime, Joe, and bonus daughter Carol; blessed grandmother to Melia, Dani, Ava, Gavin, Cody, and Jessica; and great grandmother to Colyn. Raised in Ferguson, Missouri, Karen resides in a community outside of St. Louis. Martie, a rescued Yorkie, completes her family.

———◇———

 Bobbi Linkemer is a writing coach, ghostwriter, and editor, as well as the author of nineteen books under her own name. Her eight most recent titles are on various aspects of writing. Since 2007, she has guided twenty-five authors through writing, publishing, and promoting their nonfiction books.

Bobbi's passion is helping writers to become authors through book coaching, ghostwriting, editing, online courses, and books on writing (all available in e-book format):

- *How to Write a Nonfiction Book: From planning to promotion in 6 simple steps*

- *Going Solo: How to Survive & Thrive as a Freelance Writer*

- *Words to Live By: Reflections on the writing life from a 40-year veteran*

- *The Savvy Ghostwriter: Confessions of an invisible Author*

- *How to Write an Online Course: From concept to completion, one step at a time*

- *The Book of Five: Everything authors need to know about nonfiction books*

- *The Skillful Writer: What separates the pros from the amateurs*

- *The Prosperous Author: The business of writing books*

Bobbi has been part of the St. Louis writing community for more than forty-five years, and has since moved to Florida to retire. During her long career she has been a magazine writer and editor, a corporate communicator, a marketing manager, a creator of training programs, and a mentor to other writers.

Contact Karen & Bobbi at www.ContactsConnectionsCollaboration.com 314-968-8661 or 314-503-6376

Updated manuscript by Shelly Snow Pordea

Shelly Snow Pordea is a novelist, screenwriter, and self-publishing coach. Her first novel, *Tracing Time* is consistently in the top 100 time travel romance books on Amazon Kindle and her children's book, *The Hug Who Had No Arms*, debuted as a #1 Amazon bestseller. Shelly is a speaker and cult survivor having appeared on various podcasts discussing what life and recovery after growing up in a cult is like. As a screenwriter, a fictional adaptation for a series drama of Shelly's personal story is currently in production collaboration with her brother and actor, Jon Snow. *The Tracing Time Trilogy* is currently in production development for movie adaptation.

www.shellysnowpordea.com

@shellysnowpordea

Made in the USA
Monee, IL
17 February 2023

27328233R00108